She Embraced it with Grace

True Experiences of the Pastor's Wife
Volume 1

Co-Pastor Lauretta McCoy Baldwin

SHE EMBRACED IT WITH GRACE: True Experiences of the Pastor's Wife.

Please direct all copyright inquiries to: aboverubieslb@gmail.com

Paperback ISBN: 978-1-955605-90-8

Cover and Interior Design: B.O.Y. Enterprises, Inc.

Printed in the United States.

Dedication

To the pastors' wives—
The quiet warriors, the faithful encouragers, the unseen strength behind the pulpit...
This book is dedicated to you.
For every prayer whispered in secret, every tear shed in silence, every burden carried with grace,
your sacrifice does not go unnoticed.
You are the heartbeat of ministry, the steady hands behind the scenes, and the gentle voices that speak life into the weary.
May you always know how deeply you are valued, how powerfully you are called, and how beautifully you reflect the heart of God.
With love, honor, and deepest respect, this is for you.

Proverbs 31:10, 23-31
Lady Lauretta Baldwin, Co-Pastor
Love Fellowship Outreach Church
Apostle Gonnie T. Baldwin

Table of Contents

Co-Pastor Lauretta McCoy Baldwin is a native of Darlington, South Carolina. Born on August 31 and is the eldest child of four brothers (Charles, Anthony, Sidney, and Nevell). Her parents are, Deacon Streeter and Deaconess Gloria McCoy.

She obtained her bachelor's degree from Winston-Salem State University and briefly enrolled in the MBA program. She worked in Human Resources at Winston-Salem State University for nine years and has been working in the same field at UNC School of the Arts since January 2023. Although Co-Pastor, she is currently pursuing a degree in Ministry and Christian Counseling at Vintage Bible College & Seminary.

Commitment to her family is a testament to her strong familial values. She married the love of her life, Gonnie, which most know as "Joe", on March 4, 2000, at Grace Court Gazebo downtown Winston-Salem. This union, blessed by God, brought together a daughter, Curtisha, and two sons, Jamar and Joshua. They also have 9 grandchildren. (Jazmyn, ChaNiya, Elijah, Imani, Janelle, Alyjah, Alayh, Jamar and J'Kayson.

Her unwavering dedication to the youth in her community led her to unite young individuals from diverse backgrounds under the banner of "Youth Conquerors for Christ". These young ambassadors of faith would minister in song, liturgical dance, rap, and mime for various events and festivals throughout the Triad from 2009 to 2012, leaving a lasting impact on their lives.

In 2012, she joined in ministry with her husband as he founded "The Uncompromising Word of Truth Praise & Worship Center" in Winston-Salem North Carolina.

Inspired by God, motivated, and encouraged by the Holy Spirit, in 2014, she founded "Above Rubies Pastor's Wives," a ministry to support and encourage Pastor's Wives. Coming together to fellowship, inspire, encourage, pray, impart, and then end it with good physical food.

In May 2020 she walked beside her husband Apostle Gonnie Baldwin as he received the call to lead the flock of "Love Fellowship Outreach Church" in the City of Winston-Salem North Carolina, in which two ministries were merged to continue to fulfill the call that God had on his life.

Lauretta Baldwin is a wonderful wife, a loving mother, a vibrant First Lady, and the Pastor of Love Fellowship Outreach Church, Winston Salem, NC, Inc.

Acknowledgments

I want to express my deep gratitude to my heavenly Father for inspiring this vision in 2018. Although I faced challenges that required a pause, I trusted the right time would come. Meeting my new publisher on the same date as our first meeting seven years ago was powerful. Since then, everything has flowed smoothly, proving that perseverance leads to incredible outcomes.

I want to thank my handsome husband, my best friend, my Apostle who wears a suit and shoes like no one else can. Thank you for approving my chapter. Your strength and encouragement lift me up when times get tough. Your unwavering love motivates me. I truly love you and am grateful to have you by my side.

To the dedicated Pastors' Wives: I am deeply grateful for your inspiring contributions and the warm fellowship we share. Each of you is a blessing in my life, and I cherish the unique gifts you bring. Your wisdom and kindness have touched me profoundly, and I hold you in my heart with love.

I want to express my love for my parents, Deacon Streeter and Deaconess Gloria McCoy and my mother in-law Mother Linda Walker. They have taught me the true essence of love through their unwavering support and kindness. Their actions and compassion exemplify that.

To my handsome brothers: Charles, who I nicknamed "Headache," calls me almost every day just to bug me. My other two brothers, Anthony and Nevell, are the more laid-back ones. I love all three of you!

To my children, the beautiful and talented in all her ways Curtisha, my handsome bonus son Jeff, who was always welcoming. The preacher man baby boy who always inspires me and others, the handsome Joshua, my beautiful bonus daughter Kela, who makes him smile, and the funny never a dull moment, the other handsome son Jamar: I thank God for each of you.

To my Grands that I call my heartbeats: Jazmyn, ChaNiya, Elijah, Imani, Janelle, Alyjah, Alayh, Jamar Jr., and J'Kayson. I thank God that he gives me life to witness you all growing and prospering with purpose. I pray for more days on this earth to witness, other grands to come and weddings.

I want to express my sincere gratitude to our remarkable publisher, the soon to be, Dr. Otescia Johnson. Your unwavering support, patience, and attention to detail have guided us through this journey, helping us face challenges with confidence. Thank you for being a constant presence by our side.

To my wonderful church where love thrives: "Love Fellowship Outreach Church" MY FAMILY, who is second to none. I am deeply grateful for the kindness and warmth you've shown me and my husband since the beginning. I can't name everyone! However, the mothers my "rocks" Bishop Jeannette Vaughns of Covenant of Hope International Assemblies, always a great word and teaching, (Where are your stockings) lol. Always be a lady. To our Aunt Rosalind, Aunt Yolanda, Mr. Zach, Elder Weomie who have been with us since our ministry doors opened. Our Admin's, Dr. Hope and Adjutant Felicia for keeping us updated. Thank you, Felicia, for your Patience and Kind heart to serve and assist me. Bishop Sharla for your listening ear and prayers, Cuz Elder Val for sticking with me. Elder Tomlin for trying to do everything. (sit down somewhere). As we all journey together in faith, I hold onto Romans 8:28, reminding us that all things work together for good (y'all know the rest). Your support has been a guiding light, and I cherish the bond we are creating. I just heard Keda say "Retta" sounding like Gonnie. No one can call me like her.

Chapter 1

He Hid Me in the Cleft of the Rock

Co-Pastor Baldwin

Exodus 33:21-23 *"21 And the Lord said, "Here is a place by Me, and you shall stand on the rock. 22 So it shall be, while My glory passes by, that I will put you in the cleft of the rock, and will cover you with My hand while I pass by. 23 Then I will take away My hand, and you shall see My back; but My face shall not be seen."*

Ephesians 2:10 says *for we are God's handiwork, created in Christ Jesus to do good works, which God prepared in advance for us to do.*

Listen! Co-Pastor, First Lady! Bishop, Apostle etc.… If your husband is the Senior Pastor, then you are a Pastor's Wife, an elect lady or First Lady. We have our own beliefs and have our preferences in what our members or friends around us call us and you have that right. However, no matter how many years you've been in ministry or how accomplished you are don't forget to reach over and help another Pastors Wife. Notice that I didn't say reach down to pull one up but reach over.

Life's journey can be challenging at times, and during these moments, it is crucial that we uplift and empower one another. As long as we are believers of Christ, let's set aside our reformations and denominations and come together in mutual support. Just as not all apples on the tree ripen at once, each of us has our own pace in this journey. Some may take a little longer, but rest assured, in due time, we will all flourish.

Every Pastor's Wife embodies a unique greatness that deserves to be recognized. We must strive to see them through God's loving eyes. While some may feel shy, others may experience nervousness or fear when it comes to stepping out to teach or engage in programs beyond their church community. Let us encourage and uplift them, helping them embrace their incredible potential.

Believe it or not a lack of confidence or insecurities was one of the areas I dealt with. I tried to hide it, but as we know, you get tired of putting on that mask daily. I started to really dive in the word of God and learning from great women of God around me, Apostle Gloria Samuels, Dr. Cynthia Dixon, Dr. Sandra Ingram, my mother in-law Lady Linda Walker and most of all My Mother Gloria McCoy and many more. The profound messages these women shared with me shaped my journey, guiding me to wholeheartedly embrace my authentic self. It took some time to get there but I strive to remain true to who I am, refusing to let the burdens of life's pressures and expectations disrupt my relationship with Christ. Instead, I focused on becoming the person He

11

designed me to be, showcasing my best self with genuine confidence. In doing so, I find freedom and joy in my walk of faith, knowing that I am fulfilling my purpose alongside those He has placed in my life.

Let me tell you when this title "First Lady" was added to the beginning of my name. I remember the day so clearly in the year 2012. I was in the bedroom, and I heard him call my name twice "Retta" as he came down the hall. He's normally quiet when he comes in, not saying much because he's winding down from work. This day was different, I could tell by the way he called my name. My eyes were staring at the doorway of our bedroom as I was waiting for him to turn the corner. He looked at me with stretched eyes and a half-smile and said, "Well I heard God so clear today, God has called me into Pastoral Leadership." As a wife, the most likely thing to do was sound supportive and give a positive response like "praise God". However, I just stood there in silence and finally said, "What!" with my scrunched-up face and eyes. and said, "Are you sure?" He said, "Of course I'm sure, I know when God is speaking."

The story continued with him explaining the encounter with the Lord in the kitchen at his job. He often called it his sanctuary because he was an Executive Chef (I use to call it Egypt, before he started in Ministry). His position of Youth Pastor was enough work, at least that was my thought. But who was I to question this call on his life? I was just having a moment, and my emotions were all over the place. And I know what you're thinking. You couldn't see the call of God on your husband's life? Yes, I could see the calling on his life. However, I did not expect him to come home and reveal his calling so quickly.

I had complete faith in his relationship with God, reminding myself of our favorite scripture used all the time, Romans 8:28: "And we know that all things work together for good to those who love God, to those who are called according to His purpose." This verse highlights God's divine plan and His choice in whom to favor. I recognized his deep passion for God's word, and I was determined not to do anything that could compromise this important assignment.

I started researching books and resources because I wanted to be the perfect First Lady, and I couldn't help but laugh a little as I wrote this sentence. (perfect ok Lauretta). Unlike today, there were no programs, local conferences, or books available to offer guidance. Either I didn't know where to look, or there simply wasn't much out there. I found myself reflecting on the first ladies I admired and was around at the time, envisioning myself in their shoes and believing that I could succeed with God's strength.

My husband expressed the first month that he was only going to preach on Sunday and teach Bible study during the week, and I would be left with the rest of the responsibilities. I was excited at first because I was very active for 8 years when we were leaders at my father-in-law's church, however I did have help. My handling of everything quickly changed because I would come home every Sunday feeling frustrated and upset about something. I wanted everything to be perfect, and whenever things didn't go my way, I would complain because I was tired. Yes, those humble beginnings. I would frustrate him because he didn't care about all the things such as the beautification of the church, offering envelopes, offering baskets come the foyer or even how his office was decorated. He just wanted to preach God's word, pray for the people and go home. Of course, that quickly changed to as he started helping where needed.

As First Ladies, we hold a profound responsibility to support our husbands in their esteemed roles and allow them to Pastor and guide whether its men, women, or children. As I Peter 4:8 says, "Above all, love each other deeply, because love covers a multitude of sins".

In these trying moments, Pastors may misinterpret our actions and view us as misguided, jealous or even adversarial. However, it is crucial to recognize the invaluable role of discernment, intuition, and straightforward common sense in navigating these complexities. Pastors often get a lot of attention, a spotlight that can be both compelling and overwhelming. If they struggle to manage this, they may encounter themselves having to answer questions or, worse, witness their admirable efforts or to plainly put it, their good evil spoken of.

I remember a conference we attended separately, to see Sheryl Brady. I left early with others to get good parking and seats. My husband arrived later with some other men from church and due to seating had to sit on the other side of the church. Cheryl Brady was amazing as always, and the atmosphere was charged with the Lord's presence that when she gave the alter call the people were walking up. I had a double take, it was my husband, and he kneeled on the steps, almost lying down. As a Pastor, I admired the courage it took for him to step forward. I never questioned that day, I felt a deep empathy and tears filled my eyes, which made me love him even more. In that moment, I recognized his strength feeling pride in his vulnerability and openness to God. (I finally asked him about that night today and the fact that he didn't care who saw him in this big church, knowing that most knew him. He stated when God spoke, and he had to be obedient and no one had a heaven or hell to put him in and he needed to answer to God that night.)

One day as I cruised down Highway 52, the familiar sights of Winston-Salem, NC, framed my commute to work, a routine part of my life here. The anointed voices of some of my favorite artists rang out on the radio as my thoughts, drifted back to Bishop Minny Worthy saying to me "you have the best of him now" a smile formed in my heart and on my face. To hear her say this and to be where we are now, I'm forever grateful to God And know that my husband has the best of me as well. The bible says in II Corinthians 5:17, If any man be in Christ, he is a new creature: old things are passed away; and behold all things are become new. We are in our "NEW SEASON". From the pulpit my husband often, states "I'm happy she didn't give up on this fool that didn't know better" and I always tell him that "neither of us are perfect but we're perfect for each other" in which God can use us for his Glory.

God, in His boundless mercy, forgave me and filled my life with grace, allowing me to break free from the burdens of my past mistakes and embrace a journey of healing and redemption. Because of my love for him, I chose to extend the same grace to my husband that God has graciously given to me, enabling him to carry out the divine purpose that God has laid on his heart., and the fact that he spoils me, and has what I call a "Kingdom Swag" I like, always smell good and; he has an undeniable sense of style. He even irons his T-shirts that nobody can see. However, most of all he loves the Lord. The Bible says in Isaiah 40:31 But they who wait for the Lord shall renew their strength; they shall mount up with wings like eagles; they shall run and not be weary; they shall walk, and not faint" "God revealed to me the gift He had placed in my husband and showed me the man he was destined to become. The waiting period was challenging, and not every woman can endure but God gives us the grace and strength to bear."

I heard God say so clearly, ***"I hid you in the cleft of the rock"*** I know He covered me with His hand. He passed by me often so that He could let me feel His glory and know that He was with me always. God never said or promised life would be easy, but what He did was promise He would always be with us. He wouldn't let me throw in the towel because He would have thrown it back to me. God had already revealed to me, "When I called him, I called you to walk beside him." We have to remember, our sacred walk is to actively support our husband on his ministry journey, recognizing that our involvement is crucial not only for his success but also for the fulfillment of his calling. We must continue to provide heartfelt encouragement, always covering him in prayer. As his spouse, we hold a unique position and together, creating a strong foundation empowering each other every step of the way.

One of our greatest blessings is that our children and grandchildren are actively involved in our church. Even though a couple of them have gone on to college and the dynamics have changed a bit, their participation provides them with a strong foundation in faith and helped to build their relationships with Christ. They will remember the teachings from the children's church, their experiences singing in the choir and on the Praise Team, serving in ministry, and the love they received during that time.

I know now that everything we go through has a purpose, and as I preached years ago, maybe around 2015, and my sister Lady Penny Hauser likes to say, "IT WAS NECESSARY." and I add "THERE WAS PURPOSE IN IT" which will be revealed in the right season. These moments empower us to cultivate strength and wisdom, which we can use to honor God and embrace the unique purpose He has created for each of us that can lead us to uncover our true potential and strengthen our faith along the way!

Remember: God doesn't just call one; He calls both. When He strengthens your husband, He's also preparing you to soar beside him.

Reader Journal Prompt

Take a few quiet moments to reflect and answer the following questions.

1. How can you "reach over" to support another Pastor's Wife, woman in ministry, or sister in faith this week?

_____

_____

_____

_____

2. What area of your calling do you feel God is asking you to step into with greater confidence and grace?

_____

_____

_____

_____

3. Reflect on a time when waiting on God brought transformation in your marriage, ministry, or personal walk with Him.

_____

_____

_____

_____

Chapter 2

Why Me, Why Not Me

By: C.P.R.

The story you're about to read is a spiritual battle between "Why me?" and "Why not me?" It journeys through childhood hurts, teenage pain, and the growth and maturity that come in adulthood. This story reflects not only my life but also God's divine plans and strategies for each of us. What we didn't appreciate then, we can now see through the eyes of grace. It's about conquering life's diverse challenges, fighting for victory over the enemy, and discovering who you truly are to and in God.

As you read, keep an open mind and spirit, knowing that this could have been, or may even be, your story too. You were created with purpose, called by God, and though your walk may feel lonely at times, His divine love is always beside you. It is like footprints in the sand, reminding you that you never walk alone.

Being born into this world is a blessing from God. To have life and have it more abundantly is a gift. I would later come to understand what those words truly mean. When you transition from an unsaved life to being saved, you might assume that once you accept Christ, everything becomes easy and all your worries disappear. But instead, you quickly learn the battle has just begun. You cry out, "Why me?" and God answers, "Why not you?"

I never truly understood that phrase until I grew into spiritual maturity and began to grasp God's will for my life. As a little girl, long before puberty or the understanding of right from wrong, I lived freely, swinging on playground swings, the wind blowing through my ponytails, my shoulders light and carefree. I didn't realize that being called by God at a young age also meant being targeted by the enemy. The battle wasn't mine to fight, but it was pain I had to bear. I looked to my protectors for safety, believing their love would keep me from harm, but in the blindness of being unsaved, I was unsafe.

There was a spiritual target on my back from an early age. Looking back now, I can see how the devil tried to destroy God's purpose in many young lives before it could fully bloom. I used to wonder why God would allow so much pain. Why did He let it happen? And again, He would whisper, "Why not you?"

Anger filled my heart. I cried, "Why did You let them hurt me? Why didn't You protect me? Why didn't anyone believe me when I spoke up to expose the devil? Why did You leave me feeling so defenseless and alone?" As tears ran down my face, I looked to the heavens and cried again, "Why me?" And once more, He answered, "Why not you?"

Growing up with unsaved parents who were influenced by darkness, I saw worldly possessions valued more than matters of the heart. But as the years went on, I began to feel a shift, a fresh wind of renewal from God. The sun warmed my face again. My smile returned. Love was in the air, and for the first time, I felt free.

I had reached a spiritual age where I could forgive both those who hurt me and myself for the things I had done. With God's strength, I welcomed family back into my heart. I truly believed the man in my life was sent by God, not realizing that the devil sends people too.

Through the ups and downs of life, I thought I had found the love that would fill the void from my fatherless past. He looked good, sounded good, dressed good, and even smelled good. That is how it began, looking with my natural eyes instead of my spiritual ones. But because of my history of abuse, anything that glittered like gold caught my attention. And from that "gold," came a little gold nugget. I was pregnant.

My mind filled with images of what couples do, picking baby names, celebrating holidays, and building a family. But those dreams were only fantasies. What I thought was gold turned out to be a worthless rock that sank my heart once again. All the loneliness and pain from my past came rushing back. I prayed for God to remove this cup from me. I didn't want to be a single parent. I felt ugly, unworthy, and ashamed. I envied every pretty woman I saw, believing if I were smaller or prettier, maybe my "gold" wouldn't have left.

I was so consumed by grief that I couldn't hear God whisper, "You are wonderfully made." Instead, I cried, "Why me?" and again, He answered, "Why not you?"

As time passed, I still didn't understand my worth. One "gold" led to another, and another. I eventually realized that not everything that glitters is gold. I was chasing something only God could provide. When my search was over, I had six nuggets, my children. Though I was filled with regret, I knew I had to press forward. My children were watching, and I needed to show them what strength in God looked like. I wanted them to know that He could look past our faults and flaws and still help us in our time of need.

My "golden days" were over. I had no desire for a mate; I just wanted to raise my treasures and love on the Lord. Yet even through my mistakes, I often felt empty inside. But my six nuggets, my treasures, gave my life meaning. Surrounded by family love and the support of my children's grandparents, I felt God smiling on me again, giving me a fresh start. But that peace was short-lived.

I thought the nightmare was over, but when pain touched my child the same way I had once been hurt, I screamed, "No, God! Please, not my child!" I questioned myself. How didn't I see it? How could this happen under my roof? The devil always works within the circle, and when I realized what had happened, rage consumed me. But I refused to be silent. I would not repeat the sins of silence that protected my abusers. Even knowing I might lose everything, I cried to heaven, "Why me?" and once again, He replied, "Why not you?"

The pain was unbearable. When the truth came out and the devil's works were exposed, anger overtook me. I surrendered to darkness and acted out of vengeance. I was judged not by my heart but by a broken system. Even then, God whispered His word: "Those who live by the sword, die by the sword." From my lowest place, I cried out for mercy.

Behind six-by-six walls, all I had was Jesus. In that stillness, I finally surrendered. He washed me clean and renewed my mind. When you've fallen as low as you can, the only direction left is up. In that solitude, God untangled my thoughts from Satan's influence. I began to feel joy again, light, peace, and freedom. Tears of gratitude filled my eyes as I looked back over my life and realized that through every wrong, every pain, and every loss, God had kept me.

He turned my mourning into dancing. I finally understood that He had equipped me for His glory. His love is truth. His love is strength. His love is power. And in that moment, I silenced the enemy and became a true disciple of God.

God smiled on me. I found a job, a new home, and a new car. I stood tall, no longer needing validation from any "gold." People called me a "God freak," and I accepted that proudly. I served faithfully, studied His Word, and grew in ministry until God elevated me to preach and teach the gospel. My children grew into strong, independent jewels, and God blessed us abundantly.

After fifteen years of walking faithfully, I was in a good place with God. Then, unexpectedly, someone came into my life, a leader in ministry. Because we were like-minded and equally yoked, I let my guard down. But once again, Satan came disguised as an angel of light. I stumbled, but this time, I knew the difference. A fumble doesn't mean the game is over. You can recover and still reach the finish line.

I cried out to God, ashamed and questioning my call. But Jesus spoke gently, "I am the God who sees all and knows all. I forgive you. Be not condemned. You are my child and always will be. Go and sin no more."

His mercy overwhelmed me. After exposing the deception, I forgave the one who wronged me, because judgment is not in what others do to us, but in how we respond. God restored me once again.

As I continued to serve, God called me into new territories. I saw things in His house that broke my heart, but He reminded me, "Stay until I release you." To leave too soon would be disobedience. So, I endured, trusting that joy would come in the morning.

Then, God surprised me again with a husband, a bishop. It wasn't me waiting for him; he had been waiting for me. God had to heal and prepare me first. Every scar, every tear, and every trial had purpose. He said, "I left your scars not to keep you bound but to remind you of where I brought you from."

And now, when I ask, "Why me?" God smiles and says, "Who else, if not you?"

So, to you reading this, when storms come, when you feel misunderstood or alone, remember that God is building His kingdom in you. He must do it His way, not yours. Fast, pray, study His Word, and go deeper. Because He loves you.

Miracles, signs, and wonders await. So, when you ask, "Why me?" God answers, "Why not you?"

"Just trust Me," says God.

My answer will always be, "Yes, Lord. Amen."

Reader Journal Prompt

Take a few quiet moments to reflect on your own *"Why me?"* moments.

1. What painful experiences in your life are now revealing God's purpose or protection?

   _____
   _____
   _____
   _____

2. How has God transformed your "why me" into a "why not me" testimony?

   _____
   _____
   _____
   _____

3. Write a prayer of surrender, thanking God for the strength to endure, the grace to heal, and the courage to trust His timing.

   _____
   _____
   _____
   _____

Remember: Every scar tells a story of survival, and every "why me" can become a witness of His glory.

Demetraus C. Austin is First Lady of Union Baptist Church of Thomasville, wife of Pastor Brandon Austin, mother of two sons, Rodney and Bryce.

Lady Austin was born and raised in Winston Salem, N.C to Geraldine Jackson-Thomas and Samuel Jarvis II. Mrs. Austin is best personified as a quiet storm and a fearless prayer warrior. As a retired Licensed Cosmetologist to currently advocating healthcare through pharmaceutical practices at Novant Cancer Center, Demetraus' true passion is the well-being of others. Lady Austin believes life's journey is just as important as the destination.

Demetraus discovered hidden gifts in her talent and love of dance. Her recipe for Kingdom building is God first, faith and fervent prayers. Lady Austin exemplifies a God-fearing woman recognizing that only what's done for Christ will last. In 2021 Mrs. Austin was consecrated into diaconate ministry as a deaconess by Dr. Robert L McGowens, pastor of Greater Galilee Baptist Church serving both Winston Salem and Charlotte campuses. Serving firmly, in her role as leading Lady of Union Baptist Church, Demetraus initiated Garments of Fire Liturgical dance ministry and established Y.E.S (Yielding Empowered Sisters) a women's ministry geared to encourage, uplift and nurture women on their Christian journey. Lady Austin attributes include being a member of the United Missionary Baptist Association serving as Vice-President of the Minster's Wives and Widows Auxiliary. She also volunteers in community efforts.

Lady Demi Austin

Lady Austin favors Psalms 23:4, "yea though I walk through the valley shadow of death I will fear no evil; for thy are with me; thy rod and thy staff they comfort me." She believes God has a purpose for us all and He is not finished with her yet. Her future endeavors include pursuing a business administration degree, starting a carnal victims support group and explore book writing.

Lady A. would like for you to remember her favorite quote, "I love you and there's absolutely nothing you can do about it.

Chapter 3

More Than Heels and Hats

Lady Demi Austin

I have hope in the promises of God. Being married to a minister, I knew there would be great testimonies, moments of victory, and visible displays of God's glory. What I didn't fully understand were the great tests that would come with it.

In the beginning, I was young, vibrant, and full of faith. I was also full of flesh — strong-willed, confident on the outside, yet often uncertain within. There was no manual for this calling. No orientation for the life of a preacher's wife. No seasoned guide standing before me saying, "Here is how you carry this mantle." I learned through experience, through prayer, and through the sometimes-painful lessons of trial and error.

When God desires to use us for His glory, He often allows a Goliath to stand before our crown. My Goliath was *trust*. Not trust in God, that part I professed easily. My battle was with trusting myself. I questioned my abilities, doubted my calling, and second-guessed the gifts He had already placed within me. I often asked, "God, are You sure You meant *me*?"

Those insecurities didn't stay hidden in a corner of my heart. They spilled into every area of my life, friendships, family, ministry, and even my marriage. I would pray for God to teach me to trust people, only to face more disappointment. I mistook temporary encouragement for true support and shallow words for real compassion. I was searching for validation from others when God had already stamped His approval on me.

Over time, the cracks in my trust began to show. Our marriage faced moments that felt like the very edge of breaking. It was there, in that near-death moment of our relationship, that God revealed a truth I had ignored: I was carrying my own weight, my own gift, and my own oil. I could no longer hide behind my husband's calling or his faith. God was calling *me* to stand on my own, to rise in my identity, and to walk in the anointing He had given me long before anyone called me "First Lady."

I remember when the Holy Spirit whispered Psalm 37:3-4 into my spirit: "Trust in the Lord and do good; dwell in the land and befriend faithfulness. Delight yourself in the Lord, and He will give you the desires of your heart."

For the first time, I realized that trusting God wasn't about Him re-wrapping my husband's gift and presenting it to me again. It wasn't about Him fixing what I thought was broken in someone else. It was about Him reshaping *me*. My focus had been misplaced. I wanted God to prove something to me, when He was really trying to *grow something in me*.

Still, I wrestled. My heart wanted to surrender, but my pride wanted to lead. I tried to micromanage my husband's ministry, thinking I was being helpful when, in truth, I was just afraid of being left behind. Every time I compared my contribution to his, I diminished my own worth. Every time I doubted my voice, I silenced the message God had placed in me.

Eventually, God stripped away my distractions; the opinions of others, the pressure to perform, the constant need to appear "perfect." In the silence, I heard Him more clearly. The Holy Spirit began to minister to my heart, addressing not only my insecurities but the root of them. He showed me that my distrust of others came from my distrust of myself.

I had forgiven many people in my life, but I had never truly forgiven *me*. I quoted Colossians 3:13 to others, "Forgive as the Lord forgave you," but I never applied it to my own heart. How could I help others heal when I hadn't fully accepted God's healing for myself?

That realization changed everything. I stopped fearing loss and started fearing only the loss of His presence. My greatest desire became staying in alignment with His will, even if it meant walking alone. Once I released my fear of failure, I began to walk in freedom. My confidence returned, not the kind rooted in outward appearances, but the kind anchored in God's Word and His unwavering promises.

From that moment forward, my relationship with God deepened. My prayers shifted from "Lord, fix them" to "Lord, refine me." My heart softened, my perspective changed, and my love for ministry became pure again.

Being a First Lady is not about titles, seats, or status. It is not about fancy hats, beautiful shoes, or polished public appearances. It is about living a life that reflects Jesus in every season. It is a sacred calling to love, to serve, to forgive, and to hope.

I have learned that God's promises are not limited to the pulpit or the pews. They show up in quiet moments of prayer, in unexpected blessings, and in the strength to keep standing when you feel unseen. His promises never fail. He promised to *provide*, and He has. He promised to *protect*, and He still does. He promised to *be present*, and even in my loneliest moments, He has never left me.

Now when I speak of hope, it's not wishful thinking. It's anchored faith. Hope that endures trials, hope that grows through pain, and hope that believes even when life doesn't make sense.

I understand now that every challenge I faced. I understand that every tear, every test, every Goliath was not meant to destroy me, but to develop me. Each one brought me closer to my true purpose and deeper into God's promises. And today, I walk not only as a First Lady, but as a woman who trusts, believes, and hopes completely in the Lord.

Reader Journal Prompt

Take a few quiet moments to reflect on the questions below.

1. What "Goliath" has God allowed in your life to prepare you for your crown?

_____
_____
_____
_____

2. In what areas do you find it hardest to trust God or yourself? What might He be teaching you through that struggle?

_____
_____
_____
_____

3. Reflect on a time when God's presence sustained you more than any person's validation could. What did you learn about His promises?

_____
_____
_____
_____

Remember: Hope isn't just believing God can. It's resting in the fact that He will, in His perfect time, for His perfect purpose.

Lady Annette Hairston – A Voice of Encouragement and Strength

Lady Annette Hairston is a devoted pastor's wife, a beacon of inspiration, and a woman committed to uplifting others on their journey through life. With a heart full of compassion and a voice filled with wisdom, she encourages those around her to embrace their worth, step beyond fear, and rise above intimidation.

Her path has been one of growth and perseverance—learning to overcome obstacles that once held her back, she now empowers others to do the same. Through words of encouragement and acts of kindness, Lady Annette reminds everyone she encounters that they matter, that their voices deserve to be heard, and that their potential is limitless.

As she strives to become the best version of herself, she leads by example, showing that transformation is possible when faith and determination walk hand in hand. Her presence is not just felt—it's known, cherished, and respected. This chapter explores her journey, her triumphs, and the impact she continues to make in the lives of many.

Chapter 4

I Matter

Lady Annette Hairston

The first day of becoming a Pastor's Wife was an excited and scary commitment I was not ready to take on. Everybody has this Ideal of what they think a Pastor's Wife should be doing and how they should act or carry themselves. I felt the need to present myself according to others' expectations, which was not successful for me. This position was intimidating, overwhelming, and the expectations were exhausting. I got to a place where I lost my identity of who I was and replaced my calling with a Title as a Pastor Wife, a mother, a daughter, or somebody Sister, not who God called me to be and the sad thing about it is I allowed it. Nobody sees you as your true self. We pretend to go through life accepting the call or Title man place on us, but not the Call GOD designed for us as Women.

I allowed my emotions and fear to take control of me. I lost sight of myself and not having the confidence to standup for me or better yet who GOD called me to be. Growing up I was very shy, afraid to speak up, fearful of being different and felt rejected. Just feeling like you are not enough. Just going through the motion. Someone once told me I had let myself go… that I was no longer attractive. That broke something within me. I no longer wanted to live. I wanted to leave and never come back. I knew I had to make a change, I knew Something had to Break within me. I have been in this Ministry for over 22 plus years. Even though it broke something within me it also woke something within me. I needed to make a change for me, not for anyone else. I needed to change my perspective of Me, to know that I MATTERED! I needed to see me the way God see me not the way Man sees me. Man sees you from a natural perspective, but GOD sees you from the heart, from the inside out. 1 Samuel 16:7(NIV).

Transforming Yourself

First, I needed to transform my mind. The word tells us in Romans 12:2(KJV) And be not conformed to this world: but be ye transformed by the renewing of your mind, that ye may prove what is that good, and acceptable, and perfect, will of God. I had to renew myself through His Word. Accept who God called me to be.

Secondly, I had to stop walking in Fear, for God's Word tells us in 2 Timothy 1:7 (KJV) For GOD has not given us the spirit of fear, but of Power, and of Love and a Sound Mind. I had to remind myself that God did not give us a Spirit of fear, that comes from the enemy. He gave us ALL Power to overcome the enemy with Love and do it with a Sound Mind. Even if we are afraid, do it afraid anyway.

The last thing was I had to be F.L.Y, meaning to First Love Yourself. When you truly decide to First Love Yourself it is not as easy as we think. Learn to be ok with who you are. Learn that it is ok to be different, it is ok to let go of people, family, and friends, even though people may not accept you for who you truly are. My mentor taught me to become the best version of myself and most of all Speak your truth. Always remember you have a VOICE even when people do not agree with you, laugh out loud, and dance when everyone is looking. Have fun by yourself and Most of all Forgive yourself in everything. Let it all go and know it is ok to start over. It is the most amazing thing to be F.L.Y. Why? because you matter!

A Voice

Some Women do not have a platform to use their voice or to speak their Truth. This is an important part of our Ministry in and outside of the church.

The Love for the Ministry

The things that I Love about the ministry is First is Serving. Serving came natural to me. I felt secure in helping someone else with their needs. I learned a lot about serving while I was at my home church, not just serving in the choir or ushering, but through missionary work. Tending to the needs of others was fulfilling. Second is Prayer, I learned so much through prayer and how to pray, and what to pray for and why prayer is so important for us. For me it gives me a way of escape, a peace that surpasses all understanding also a Love for God's word.   last is the beautiful people you meet along the way. In this Ministry it can really get lonely along the way, especially for a Pastor's Wife. So, when God places someone in your life that you can identify with or know the shoes you walk in it becomes a comfort to know you are not alone on this journey and you can encourage or be encouraged along the way even if it is just for a season.

Pastor's Wives

I want to encourage every Pastor Wife to know that you Matter. We are so much more than the Suits and the Hats we wear. We are so much more than the shoes on our feet or sitting on the front row. We are called to do a work for God. Ephesians 2:10 (KJV) We are created for His workmanship to inspire, encourage and love our sisters in Christ, but most of all the ones not in Christ, not to tear down, but to build each other up and learn to be the lifter of their heads. Psalm 24:7-10(KVJ) Know that we are Ordained by God not man. Let us learn to be accountable for each other. Teach our mothers our daughters, our sisters to believe in each other and straighten each other's crowns especially when we are broken. Let us become the best version of ourselves one that Leaves a Legacy, build each other up and help tear down strong holds the come against us. One thing I have learn is that it is easy to see the wrong and find the faults in one another because we tend to look

40

with our natural eye, but if we start looking with our Spiritual eye, we will see the brokenness behind our pain and hurt and that causes us to act out in the natural. Too many of us have spoken judgement on one another without truly knowing what is going on from the inside out. I believe that once we know our worth, build our confidence within ourselves then we can help others along the way. It is not easy to face your truth, but it is worth it. How do I know well glad you asked. I was this person acting out not having the confidence within myself but having confidence for everyone else. Cheering everybody else on. Pouring into everybody else except myself. Giving everything within myself and not receiving the things that God had for me. Feeling that I did not deserve anything back. Always feeling empty. Afraid to ask or receive things for myself. Then I became emotionally and physically broken not wanting to talk or speak to anyone. When covid came it made it easier for me not to deal with anyone so I shutdown everybody. I saw my family falling apart and broken and I did not like what I saw in them especially within me. I knew I had to make a change within myself to help my family, so I asked God to be my therapist to help me change me seeking His counsel from there started taking a class to help me see me for the better even though I did not want to face the truth about myself but I knew I had to for myself and my family not only for them but for others who need to hear my Voice. God has a plan for your life, and we do not have to do it alone. Allow someone else to help you find your Voice and know that you Matter. I Matter. We Matter.

Reader Journal Prompt

Take a few quiet moments to reflect on the questions below.

1. In what ways have you allowed titles, roles, or expectations from others to define your worth? How can you begin to see yourself the way God sees you, from the inside out?

_____

_____

_____

_____

2. What area of your life needs transformation through the "renewing of your mind"? Write about one mindset or fear you're ready to surrender to God so you can walk boldly in your true identity.

_____

_____

_____

_____

3. How can you begin to First Love Yourself (F.L.Y.) today practically, spiritually, and emotionally? Describe one way you can use your voice or your story to encourage another woman who feels unseen or unheard.

_____

_____

_____

_____

Remember: You are not the title others give you. You are who God says you are… chosen, loved, and equipped to make a difference!

Pastor Heatherly Price is the wife of Derrick Price and mother of Derrick Jr and Malachi Josiah, step mom to 2 daughters D'Aria and Di'Andra and Mimi to 6 grands. She is also a younger sister & sister-in-law to Mandy Brunson & Bruce Brunson and an aunt to 2 nephews and 1 niece. Her parents Donald and Shirley Burton have gone on to be with the Lord. With that being said the dynamics of family and how to navigate in relationships are a place where God is always teaching her and her family to grow.

As a licensed Minister & Pastor with her husband of Restoration International Ministries in Greer SC, she wants to always be in the will of the Father. Walking in the prophetic, she always wants to ensure she hears from Jehovah God. She's an entrepreneur with her business, Vessels of Honor Jewelry, which is a ministry in itself. As the Lord allows her to create, she prays over the items created that God would minister and bless each one that wears her designs. These are just a few attributes of her life that has led her to where God has her at this point and to where God will have her to go in the future. She is trusting God in every step.

Acknowledgement

I want to first thank ABBA Father for who He is and all He has done for me and my family. I thank the Lord Jesus for His love and sacrifice, I thank the Holy Spirit for being my guide and comforter in this life as I strive to live for God. I also want to give honor to my husband Derrick for his love, support, commitment, and strength as the one that completes me in the Lord, our children and grandchildren, my mom, dad, and sister and everyone else in my life that has helped me to become the Woman of God I am today. I am truly grateful for Pastor Lauretta Baldwin for her vision for this anthology and her pushing for us to work together to accomplish this goal as well as her loving spirit to reach souls for the kingdom. I pray the testimony of God's greatness will touch hearts and lives and will minister to each one and guide souls to the saving knowledge of Jesus Christ.

Chapter 5

Appointed Experiences

Lady Heatherly Price

In every experience of life, we have to look for where God has been in it. Through both my marriage and my divorce, I came to know God as my anchor and my keeper.

When I look back now, I realize that I was spiritually naïve, even though I was saved. I was emotionally manipulated into marriage at the age of twenty. I remember coming out of one of my college classes and sitting in my car when he called. I told him I didn't think I could go through with the marriage because of how I was feeling spiritually. He told me that he was sitting with a gun, saying he couldn't live if I didn't marry him.

I sat in that car, crying, asking God if this was what I was supposed to do to save his soul. If only I had stayed the course, listened to the Holy Spirit, and followed through with my "no." Maybe things would have turned out differently.

But God, who is all-knowing and all-powerful, kept me through those thirteen years.

Not everything was bad, there were good moments, but most of it was rocky. I had to trust God through it all. Now I understand why we were never able to have children. At the time, that reality made me feel sad, bitter, and alone. I longed to experience motherhood. I watched my sister have children. I listened as my parents talked about grandchildren, and I wanted so badly to give them that joy. When it didn't happen, I buried those feelings deep inside and asked God to help me release them.

I prayed for my husband, I prayed for myself, and I prayed for our marriage. As a child of God from an early age, I knew He had called me for something greater. I wanted to serve, to minister, to be the vessel He created me to be. Yet even while I was ministering, something always felt missing. I would ask God, "What do I need to do?" I wanted to serve Him with my whole heart, mind, soul, and spirit, but somehow, I felt incomplete.

As the years went on, many situations arose in which God showed Himself mighty and strong. He allowed me to attend ministerial training classes where I met my now husband. We were just friends then, learning what it meant to serve God through ministry. We were taught that all of us were created to worship, and that message resonated deeply with me.

Still, I had to endure another year and a half before God released me from that first marriage. During that time, I was truly losing myself. As much as I wanted to serve God, I was slowly dying inside. I had lost my mother, which brought deep regret, guilt, and sadness. I felt abandoned, shattered, and unsure of who I was anymore.

As a minister, I knew I shouldn't feel this way, but I did. I prayed, I served, but I was numbing the pain in other ways. I didn't feel loved by my husband, and I began to question how God could call someone so broken. I wrestled with confusion, depression, and self-doubt. But God.

When I was at my lowest point, when everything in me was tired and torn, God sent a friend with a word of direction. They told me, "God doesn't want you to live in misery, crying for days. Let Him show you what to do."

That word shook something inside me. I began to pray differently, not for escape, but for clarity. I asked God to help me release everything to Him. Slowly, He began to reveal His plan. I realized that with His help, I could finally take the steps I had been too afraid to take.

For years, I believed that once you got married, you stayed no matter what. But I had no spiritual or emotional support, and the relationship had no desire for healing. It was built on manipulation and untruths. I was terrified to leave, yet even more afraid of dying in spirit if I stayed.

After thirteen years, I made the hardest decision of my life to walk away. I want to be clear: I do not promote divorce. But I know what it is to live through one. I learned that if you seek God earnestly, He will guide your steps. Always seek His direction before marriage. Be sure you hear His voice clearly before you say, "I do," so you don't have to walk through the kind of pain I did.

But if you are already in a situation where you have done all you can and you're still crying out for direction, trust God. He will show you what to do. I know because He did it for me.

God sent the love of my life, the man who would become my husband, partner, and pastor, during the time when I felt most broken. He showed me that there is life after divorce. There is love after divorce. And there is freedom when you trust God with your next chapter.

God's Miracle Hand

Derrick and I had only been married about three weeks when he almost lost his life. We had started exercising and playing basketball together, but during that week he began to lose weight rapidly. We thought it was just the new routine and diet changes. On Saturday evening, as we drove to the hotel for our usual weekend church service, he could barely stay awake. He had no strength and was visibly weak, but he kept saying he just needed rest.

We made it to church the next morning. Derrick looked frail. His shoes were flopping, his lips were dry, and his clothes hung loosely. We prayed through the service, asking God for direction and healing. Afterward, we went back to the hotel so he could rest. But as I watched him, I knew something was seriously wrong. I insisted we go to the hospital.

When we arrived, the nurses rushed him back immediately. The doctor soon told me he was in diabetic ketoacidosis. His blood sugar was 1,046. My heart sank. Fear rushed over me, but I prayed harder. I refused to believe that the man God had just joined to me would be taken so soon.

The next five days were filled with fear, tears, and faith. We prayed, we cried, and we trusted God. When Derrick was released, we knew his healing journey would take time. It has been a process, but through it all, we've continued to trust God as our Keeper and Deliverer.

Four years later, we faced another terrifying moment that reminded us again of God's miracle-working hand. Derrick had an accident at work. Our boys, then five and six years old, were in bed when I got the call. Derrick told me a 10,000-pound trailer had fallen on his foot. He said the only thing he could do was pray in the Holy Spirit.

As I drove toward him, my heart pounded. I tried to keep calm for our boys in the backseat, who kept asking questions I couldn't answer. Derrick's voice on the phone was trembling, but he was still praying. When the nurse began removing his shoe, I heard her say, "I see blood." My stomach dropped. I wanted to panic, but I knew I had to stay composed for him. They took him back for examination while I drove, praying under my breath.

When I arrived, the worker who brought him in told me softly, "It isn't as good as we had hoped." My knees went weak. I had to gather my strength before going in. I told myself, *you have to be strong.* When I walked into the room, the sight of his foot stopped me. His toes were crushed and bleeding. My heart shattered, but I held my composure. I grabbed his hand and whispered, "It's okay, Baby. We're going to trust God."

The doctor told us he would need to be transferred for surgery. All five toes had to be removed. In that moment, I chose gratitude over grief. My husband was alive. And for that, I will forever be thankful.

God's miraculous hand was evident in every step. Through both of those experiences, He showed us His power to heal, His strength to sustain, and His faithfulness to deliver.

Reader Journal Prompt

Take a few quiet moments to reflect on the questions below.

1. When have you seen God's hand sustain you through a painful or frightening experience? How did He show Himself faithful?

_____

_____

_____

_____

2. What lessons have you learned about trusting God's direction, especially in relationships or life decisions?

_____

_____

_____

_____

3. How has God's restoration in one season prepared you to walk with greater faith in the next?

_____

_____

_____

_____

Remember: Even when life breaks you, God never leaves you. His miracle hand can rebuild, restore, and renew every part of your story.

Lady Tujuana Bailey Barr is married to Bishop Gordon Barr and is a member of the Kingdom Movers Ministries Outreach, located in Winston-Salem, NC. We have one daughter, Ms. Denasha Harding and three grandchildren, Tyrione, Zyrione, and Dehari'. She is the daughter of Mr. Michael Thomas and Ms. Belinda Bailey. Lady Barr accepted Christ at the age of 8yrs old and became a member of the Oak Grove Missionary Baptist Church, located in the city of Walkertown, NC, where the Pastor was the late Rev. Ira L. Anthony. She served on various committees, worked in the music ministry as the director of choir, the social committee, and served in the Sunday School Department for twenty plus years. Last year, Lady Barr accepted the call into Ministry in June 2024.

Lady Barr is currently working at the Novant Health Clemmons Medical Center in Clemmons, NC and has been employed with Novant Health in the Nursing field for over 27years. She is currently studying at ECPI University in their Healthcare Administration, Master's Degree Program and will be graduating in December 2025. Lady Barr loves to shop, travel and sing. But most of all, she loves the Lord and is a Women of God. She loves to serve and help those in need and has a heart for the people. Two of her favorite scriptures are Proverbs 3:5-6 and Philippians 4:13.

Acknowledgement Page

I would first like to give thanks to my Lord and Savior for blessing me with the opportunity to be part of this incredible journey alongside such beautifully created women, each contributing their voices to the Pastor's Wives Book.

I also extend my deepest gratitude to my husband, my Bishop, Bishop Gordon Barr, for his unwavering love and support throughout this process. Your encouragement has been invaluable.

Thank you to my mother as well for all of her genuine love and support that she has given me over the years. She always encourages me and lets me know that I can do it and she has my back.

Lastly, I want to honor my Spiritual parents, Apostle Baldwin and Pastor Lauretta Baldwin, for their vision and dedication. Thank you for allowing us to help bring this divine calling to fruition. I am truly grateful!

Lady Tujuana Bailey Barr

Chapter 6

Bitten But Blessed

Lady Tujuana Barr

As a child growing up in the Vargrave area of Winston-Salem, NC, I was living with my grandmother because my mother was in college, and she had me when she was 18 years old. My grandmother told my mother that she was going to finish college and not to worry that I would be just fine. See, my mother and father were high school sweethearts, and they never married, so you know what that means. Yes, I am the only child. No, I am not spoiled but my mother and grandmother let me know that I was going to work for whatever I wanted because nothing is free.

At a young age, I was in Vacation Bible School and my late Pastor, Rev. I. L. Anthony, whom was the Pastor at Oak Grove Missionary Baptist Church, in Walkertown, NC, was up giving the invitation and the next thing I knew, I found myself walking toward the front of the church, ready to give my life to the Lord at the age of eight years old. A few weeks later, I was Baptized. My Pastor dipped me down in that cold water and when I came up, I found out that I was a New Creature in Christ. Ready to serve the Lord, I had a zeal for God that all I wanted to do was help somebody, all I wanted to do was show love, and serve the Lord at such a young age.

I started inviting my friends to come to church with me and I started telling them about Jesus, but it was up to them, if they wanted to follow him or not. I continued to work in the church as I grew up. My grandmother made sure that I was not going to miss a service, and if I was up late, you best believe she was going to wake me up for service. All through school, I remained active in church, sang in various choirs, attended Sunday school, worked in the nursery, and in the Youth Department.

One day, I was in the eighth grade, I woke up and wasn't feeling well and I told my mother that I was sick and needed to stay home for the day. I was hurting, I couldn't hold any food down and I was like that for two or three days and my grandmother told my mom to get me out of this house and take her to the doctor. My mother had made me an appointment and the next thing I know I was at my pediatric doctor at the age of 13 and I had dehydrated on the table and my urine was bloody and the doctor told my mother that I needed to be rushed to the hospital and my mother said that she would take me, no need to wait for an ambulance. I arrived at Brenner's Children Hospital and had to have emergency surgery, my appendix had ruptured, and I had poison spread all over my system and the surgeon came out to tell my family that there was nothing else that they could do for me, that they had never seen a case as bad as this one and my family immediately began to pray in the hospital lobby. I came through the surgery all right. I had an NG tube, IV's, and all I could eat was ice chips. The surgeons had left my incision open in case they had to operate on me again. A

55

week later, I ended up having another surgery, they removed one of my ribs and placed tubes on my right side so that the poison could continue to drain. I had to stay in the hospital for 30 days, my family came to feed me ice chips, prayed with me and supported me around the clock for those 30 days. When I was feeling better, I told Dr. Parker, who was my surgeon at the time that I was ready to go home. A few days later I was home with home care and recovering well. I was bitten but blessed.

As I was recovering, I had home schooling because I was out for a long time because they did not want me to contract an infection. I remained faithful in my schoolwork, and I ended up passing eighth grade with honors. The next school year I was going to be a freshman at Carver High School. The devil thought he had me, but he didn't realize that I had been bitten but I was still blessed.

As I was preparing for my nineth grade school year, I looked different. I had a new hairstyle because I lost some of my hair because of anesthesia and I had lost so much weight that my mom had to purchase a new wardrobe for me. See despite my sickness, I remained faithful in God's word. I still served him and continued to press my way into church, even when I wasn't feeling well, but I was there.

While I was continuing to grow in the things of God and in my education, and I graduated from Carver High School and went on to college. During my freshman year at NC A&T State University, I found myself starting to go in a different direction than what I was supposed to do. My grades were dropping, I was hanging out with my friends, I had a car, so we were going to different parties and hanging out and the next thing I know, my mom was there packing up my things and bringing me back home. I lost my scholarship, and I had to decide what I was going to do now. I was bitten but blessed.

See every now and then we as Christians must have a reset. Now that doesn't mean stopping everything, there might be a small delay, but it wasn't denied. In my early twenties I had to have a refresher, I had to get my head on straight as the older saints used to say. I had to figure out what I was going to do with myself, so I started working at Hecht's Department Store part-time and I was attending Forsyth Tech to take some college courses and to figure out what I wanted to do. Then it came to me, I loved helping others and I remembered how they helped me when I was in the hospital. So, after praying, I decided to sign up for CNA classes. I figured that I could get my feet wet with that and see if that was really what I wanted to do. I completed all the necessary classes and passed. I received my CNA license and started applying for jobs. The first job that called me was Forsyth Memorial Hospital and a few weeks later I was working daytime on second general. I was bitten but blessed.

A few years later, I completed my courses at FTCC and started taking nursing classes at UNCG. I was commuting daily and still working but I was working the night shift, seeing home health patients and going to school. At the age of thirty, I had saved enough money and entered a first-time home buying program with ERC and the next thing I know I was signing the papers on my new home. I moved out and into my own home. See as I grew older, I had to realize that I could not do anything without my heavenly father, I drew closer to him and had a closer relationship with him. I was reminded that the Lord would never put more on you than you can bear. One of my favorite scriptures is Proverbs 3:5-6, in the KJV and it reads, "Trust in the Lord with all thine heart; and lean not unto thine own understanding. In all thy ways acknowledge him, and he shall direct thy paths". I had to learn to trust in the Lord. I had two more years to go in the nursing program and the Lord called my grandmother home. I had to figure out what I wanted to do in life. Then one day my mom showed up on my doorstep, sick with pneumonia and had to be hospitalized for a few days. As she got better, she moved in with me and has been with me ever since my grandmother passed. Bitten but blessed.

As I continued to live this thing we call life, I realized that I did not want to be single anymore. I wanted a husband, someone to spend time with, take care of me and provide for me and settle down and enjoy the rest of my life with. I wanted a man that loved God more than he loved me. Not realizing that he was preparing me for a Pastor as my husband. At the time while serving in the church and working closely with my Pastor, who was also my great uncle, I often wondered why he had me doing the things that I was doing back then but I know now. He was preparing me for my future. He was preparing me for the fickle people, the backstabbing and gossiping people that had me on my knees all the time. I am so very thankful to this day for my training and experience from my home church because it prepared me for this day. Bitten but blessed.

On November 8, 2014, I married my husband that the Lord had prepared just for me. My sexy chocolate, my Boo thang, and my Bae. We had only been married for a year, and he came to me and told me that the Lord had called him to start his own ministry. I immediately began to cry and say, "Oh Lord, why me?" And the Lord says, "Why not you?" I started praying even more because I knew that the devil was not too far away because everyone is not saved. The first Sunday in December 2015, the doors of Kingdom Movers Ministries Outreach were opened, and service was held. In April of 2016, my husband was installed as Pastor. Last year, my husband was elevated to the office of Bishop. I knew then, the higher the office, the higher the hits would come, and I had to be ready for whatever came our way. This year we will be celebrating our tenth Church and Pastoral Anniversary. To God Be the Glory! Bitten but blessed.

Serving God's people is not an easy task, especially when you are a Pastor's wife. Showing love to others especially when you know they don't love you back is tough but required. Serving sometimes includes being talked about behind your back and taking the hits that were meant for your husband, but you got hit instead. Decerning spirits as they walk through the church doors and having to pray even harder for deliverance is necessary.

Sometimes you feel all alone, like there is only you. I have learned that there is not a friend like the lonely Jesus, no not one, no not one. He reminds me that I am never alone, that He will be there with me even until the end. I am very thankful for the few mentors that I had who were Pastor's wives and they prayed, guided, and advised me on several occasions, and I really appreciate them for that. I had to take my faith walk a little higher and I had to trust and depend on God a little more. There were times when my feelings hurt, and I would cry because of the hurtful words said from the saints and I had to pray and ask the Lord to protect my heart. At that time, I was leading while I was bleeding and that is not good. I had to ask the Lord to heal, deliver and set free so that I could take the blinders off and start seeing in the natural and in the spirit. And that is just what He did. I was bitten but blessed.

I want to encourage another Pastor's wife who will be reading this book, that you are not alone. Other Pastor's wives have been through the same or a similar situation like yours. I want to remind you that you are a woman of grace. You are the Proverbs 31 woman. All you must do is be who God called you to be, remember that you are a chosen generation, a royal priest hood, a holy nation. You are different, you are chosen for this season. When you walk into a room, take ownership of that room. Don't walk with your head down, know your worth. Know who you are in Christ. Establish a deeper relationship with Him. Be reminded that you just can't dress like you want to dress, you can't say what you want to say sometimes, but you must always show the love of God. You are fearfully and wonderfully made. You are the ruby; you are God's masterpiece. Stay in your word, study, and continue to allow the Lord to lead and guide you cause your steps are ordered. Bitten but blessed.

Reader Journal Prompt

Take a few quiet moments to reflect on the questions below.

1. Think about a time when life "bit" you; a challenge, setback, or heartbreak that could have destroyed your faith. How did God reveal that you were still *blessed* in the midst of it?

_____

_____

_____

_____

2. This chapter highlights seasons of preparation, moments when God was shaping you for greater purpose even when you didn't understand it. What experiences in your own life do you now recognize as preparation for where you are today?

_____

_____

_____

_____

3. The writer says, "I was leading while I was bleeding." Have you ever tried to serve others while you were still healing? How did God help you to find strength, balance, and restoration in that season?

_____

_____

_____

_____

Remember: You may have been bitten, but you are still blessed. Every scar tells a story of God's faithfulness and grace at work in your life.

Lady Lisa Hill is a Board-Certified Nurse Coach, a registered nurse, and a graduate of Winston-Salem State University with a Bachelor of Science in Nursing. I've been blessed to spend my life serving others, both in healthcare and in ministry.

I've been married for 35 wonderful years and am the proud mother of two sons, one of whom has gone on to be with the Lord. This loss has profoundly shaped my faith and continues to strengthen my walk with God. In 2016, I was ordained as an elder, a moment that confirmed my call to help others grow spiritually and emotionally.

I founded Freedom Tabernacle Family Worship Center with my husband to be a place where people can find healing, freedom, and a true sense of community. Along the way, I wrote "Hospitality Hacks: Feel Loved and At Home for Overnight Guests," a book that shares my passion for welcoming others with intentionality and heart.

Outside of work and ministry, I love spending time at home with my two dogs—Stella, a Rottweiler, and CoCo, an American Bully—and tending to my flower garden. Health and wellness are more than hobbies for me—they're a way of life. Whether I'm coaching clients, encouraging others through faith, or simply relaxing in my backyard, I aim to live each day with purpose, peace, and gratitude.

Acknowledgements

I want to express my deepest gratitude to my beloved husband, Pastor Donald A. Hill, and my wonderful son, Joshua L. Hill, for their unwavering love, support, and encouragement throughout this journey. Your strength and presence have carried me through more than words can say.

I also honor the memory of my late son, Donald A. Hill, Jr (A.J.), whose spirit continues to inspire me every day. Though he is no longer with us in body, his love lives on in our hearts and memories always.

A Funny Story in Ministry...

During one of our baptisms, we had an extremely tall candidate. The Pastor and Elder tried to be intuitive by getting him as close to the front of the baptismal pool as possible to submerge him thoroughly in the water. They gave directions on what was about to occur, but for whatever reason, there was a slight shift in the positioning as the candidate was going down in the water. The back of his head hit the wall with a loud pop sound effect. He let out, "Oh, my head," but the Pastor and the Elder holding onto him still forced him into the water, saying with a loud voice, "You going down today in the name of the Father, Son, and Holy Ghost!" I had to hand him his towel with a straight face without laughing.

Chapter 7

Thriving Where He Plants Me

Lady Lisa Hill

"The righteous shall flourish like the palm tree: He shall grow like a cedar in Lebanon. Those that be planted in the house of the Lord shall flourish in the courts of our God. They shall still bring forth fruit in old age; they shall be fat and flourishing; To shew that the Lord is upright: He is my rock and there is no unrighteousness in him." **-Psalm 92:12-15 KJV**

The Winter season of 2012 was a life-altering moment on a National level. The horrible news of the Sandy Hook school shooting was a precursor on a more intimate level in my own life of experiencing a deep, profound loss and navigating the emotions of grief. The exact date, 12-19-2012, started like any ordinary day. My oldest son, Donald Hill, Jr. aka AJ, was home for winter break. He was a junior at Howard University taking on the leadership of the Alternative Spring Break, where there is a focus on gun violence. AJ, my youngest son Joshua, my husband, and I had been enjoying family time the past week,

65

reminiscing and laughing, reminiscing how it's just like old times, not knowing life as we knew it would never be the same.

12-16-2012 AJ preached the Sunday Morning Sermon we were alone in his daddy's office, chit-chatting about being a little nervous, to which I told him God got you we hugged and prayed to calm his nerves and let God use you. I was a proud mama beaming joyfully as he engaged the congregation and challenged us to a personal relationship. He gave examples of how he had been a witness for Christ on campus to the point where they nicknamed him Reverend, Dr. Bishop, Martin Malcom Jr, yet the most endearing example was him being an instrument in restoring the relationship of a colleague and her estranged father.

My son was always intentional and supportive; 2 days before his death, AJ, Josh, and I were in the kitchen talking, and he asked the question, Mama, what if I die? The fact that I knew he was secure in his salvation, I responded, you have so much life ahead of you, getting ready to fly out to Chicago with the school president's wife in first class; you have a purpose to fulfill. Then the focus shifted to how he wanted to fly out with a blue double-breasted suit tailor-made, we joked and carried on with our shenanigans.

The night before his death, I received an injection in my knee for pain, AJ said mama, stay in that bed while I'm home. I got you, gave me a kiss, said I love you and turned off my light. That would be the final words and moment I had with my son. Upon rising the next morning, his door was cracked, and I decided I didn't want to disturb him, so off to work I went since I had a psychiatry meeting with my colleague first thing to review care plans, I left my phone at the job, and upon returning.

My husband and I had been married 22 years at this time, and he asked if I was coming home for lunch, to which I replied no, but I can. He was stern and said come home and come home now. I informed my co-worker that something was wrong and that he didn't want to tell me over the phone. Will you cover for me? While driving home, I was thinking trying to figure out what could have happened. I wondered if he shot the neighbor's dog or had an altercation with the new Rottweiler puppy we had.

As I turned into our neighborhood, there were police cars everywhere, but I was able to pull into the driveway. As I stepped out of the car, I asked the police officer what was going on. He responded I'm going to let your husband tell you. In my mind, I said you're the police, walking up the steps. My husband was coming out the front door onto the porch; his eyes were full of tears, and I had never seen him cry. I asked what was wrong. He was speechless, but talking with his eyes filled with sorrow and pain is the only way I can describe it. He finally could voice the words, AJ's gone to. To which I replied, gone where? His hands and head were shaking repeating himself. I said all these cops, they are going to find him. Realizing I did not understand the gravity of the situation, he finally said AJ was dead.

At that moment, shock and utter disbelief followed with a wailing I can't put into words. Seeing my firstborn son lying in his bed with two blood stain drops on his pillow and a peaceful look on his face gave me pain and pleasure. In that space, my husband, son, and I just hugged and cried with each other. The cops were very respectful and allowed us to express our pain, to which my baby boy stated that he didn't know how to feel, only that he was stable.

Three weeks later, my maternal grandmother and stepmother died a day apart. Our ministry, Freedom Tabernacle Family Worship Center, is still in its infancy stage of 3 years. I took 3 weeks off from church while taking 2 months away from work. I cried and cried and cried, wondering what had happened when he was healthy. We were investigated, and we learned it is a standard protocol to rule out foul play due to no reason my son should be dead from the natural standpoint. The autopsy report came back six months later to confirm his death was ruled as a heart attack.

The question was, how do you thrive in a place where God plants you? Reflecting on the bitter cup of life yet, I preach and teach others to trust God and when my crisis hit me, those words would not penetrate my own heart. I felt like an empty shell observing others who had their loved ones, and yet mine was no longer with me. Then, one day, while meditating in my thoughts, I reflected on how Hannah had prayed for a male child 1 Samuel 1:10-11 she was in bitterness of soul and prayed unto the Lord and wept sore. She vowed a vow and said, *"O Lord of host if thou wilt indeed look on the affliction of thine handmaid, and remember me, and not forget thine handmaid, but wilt give unto thine handmaid a man child, then I will give him unto the Lord all the days of his life, and there shall no razor come upon his head."*

I remember dedicating my sons to the Lord and accepting that they are only a lend from the Lord. When that shift in my perception changed, I could go longer without having meltdowns, and eventually, almost none, instead reflecting on the memories we created and shared. Suddenly, I started noticing an increase in people who would ask how I did it and were aware of my dilemma: how can you smile when something like that has happened? The answer is that my faith and hope are planted in the Lord.

If you take note of the opening scripture, it is a reminder that a child of God shall flourish no matter how deep the pain. I am not exempt from pain, and the reminder that God's only begotten son was a sacrifice for all humanity. His son died a crucial, horrific death for the sins of others. My son died in peace in the comfort of his own bed among a family that loved him. When the son of King David and Bathsheba was gravely ill for seven days he did not eat or drink but fasted, praying that the child would be healed his servants were afraid to tell him the child had died from his actions, but David perceived that the child was dead he arose from the ground stating that he can no longer come to him, but he can go to him. Those words resonate in my soul giving me the assurance and hope that we will one day reunite again. This truth allows me to Thrive where He plants me.

Reader Journal Prompt

Take a few quiet moments to reflect on the questions below.

1. This chapter reveals how grief and faith can coexist. Reflect on
    a loss you've experienced. How did God reveal His presence in
    your pain, even when you couldn't feel Him at first?

    _____

    _____

    _____

    _____

2. Lady Hill describes a moment when her perspective shifted from
    grief to gratitude, recognizing that her son was a "lend from the
    Lord." What perspective shift has God been calling you to make
    about something or someone you've had to release?

    _____

    _____

    _____

    _____

3. "Thrive where He plants you" means finding purpose even in
    broken places. What practical steps can you take today to grow
    emotionally, spiritually, or purposefully right where God has
    placed you?

    _____

    _____

    _____

    _____

Remember: Pain may visit, but purpose will always remain. Even in
loss, God's love plants seeds that will bloom again in His time.

Pastor Sandra Samuels is a dedicated servant of God, a worshipper, mentor, and virtuous woman with a heart brimming with gratitude. Her devotion to the work of the Lord radiates through her every action, and to know her is to experience a genuine, unshakable love. Humble in spirit, she often assures others that with faith and trust in God, all things are possible.

For 20 years, Pastor Samuels was married to the late Bishop Stephone Devon Samuels. Together, they co-founded Transformation Ministries, a beacon of faith where Pastor Samuels now leads the Women's Ministry with grace and compassion. In every aspect of her life, whether as a wife, mother, daughter, or friend, she honors her calling with a heart steadfast in belief. Above all, she cherishes her role as a follower of Jesus Christ, whose love and guidance have shaped her path.

Bishop and Pastor Samuels were blessed with five children and four grandchildren, filling their lives with joy and legacy. Pastor Samuels' spiritual journey began when she was baptized and received the Holy Spirit at her home church, Mt. Calvary Holy Church in Winston-Salem, NC, a place that remains close to her heart. She attended Vintage Bible College to further her biblical studies.

On August 19, 2024, Pastor Samuels was ordained as the Pastor of Transformation Ministries. Her love for the Lord is deep and unwavering. She has dedicated herself to fulfilling the mission

God has entrusted to her, walking in faith and purpose. Her favorite scripture, Psalms 23, reflects her unyielding trust in God: "I believe whatever I need, God will not only comfort me but will always provide for me."

Chapter 8

A Place Called There

Pastor Sandra Samuels

"But may the God of all grace, who called us to His eternal glory by Christ Jesus, after you have suffered a while, perfect, establish, strengthen, and settle you." -1Peter 5:10 NKJV

Most people think pastors and pastors' wives are always serious and never have a sense of humor. I want to start this chapter by saying that's 100% false. Not only do we enjoy our lives, but we also enjoy having a good time together.

A perfect example is how my husband proposed to me. I remember that day so vividly. I was driving along, minding my business, when suddenly I saw blue lights flashing in my rearview mirror. My heart immediately started racing because, like most people, seeing those lights will make you panic. I pulled over, and the officer walked up to my car and said, "Ma'am, can I see your license?"

I replied, "Sir, I wasn't going fast. I know I wasn't going more than five miles over."

He asked again for my license, so I handed it to him, still a little confused. He walked back to his car, and for a few moments, I sat there trying to figure out what I could have possibly done wrong. Then, out of nowhere, I saw my husband walking toward me — not the officer. He had the biggest smile on his face, and before I could say anything, he got down on one knee.

The officer grinned and said, "Ma'am, I'm not letting you go until you say yes."

I was in complete shock, laughing and crying all at once. I said "yes," of course, and the officer handed my license back. Later, when I got my husband alone, I let him have it — with a kiss! We laughed about it afterward, but at the time, when those blue lights first flashed, I wasn't laughing at all.

When Suffering Becomes a Teacher

Becoming my husband's wife wasn't just about sharing life together; it was a divine assignment, a Kingdom partnership. I had gone to church most of my life, but I never truly understood what trials and tribulations were until I became older. My mother would always talk about her faith, and while I respected her relationship with God, I didn't really grasp the depth of what she meant until I had to live through my own seasons of lack and loss.

There were moments when we didn't have much, yet somehow, God always provided. I didn't understand how He did it, but He did. I didn't know what true suffering was until adulthood, when my faith had to stand on its own.

I remember times when life felt unfair… when prayers seemed unanswered and the weight of responsibility pressed on every side. But through those moments, I began to realize that suffering produces strength, humility, and total dependence on God.

It was in those quiet, tearful nights that I began to understand what my mother meant when she said, "God will make a way." I learned that pain has purpose, and that purpose always points us back to the Cross.

The Place Called There

As the years passed, I began to understand that there is a place God brings us to, a place of trust, surrender, and refinement. That place is what I now call *there*.

In my journey, I gained some things and lost some things. The hardest loss of all was my husband, my best friend. The day he passed away, my entire world shifted. I remember getting the call that changed everything. I was excited about an upcoming trip we had planned, only to hear the words, "Your husband passed out."

When I arrived, I realized my life as I knew it would never be the same. The love of my life had gone home to be with the Lord.

In that moment, I felt empty and shattered. I sat in silence, crying out to God through hot tears that wouldn't stop falling. I knew my husband loved the Lord. I had no doubt about where he was spending eternity. But I also knew that my life on this side of heaven would never look the same again. The pain was unbearable, yet it was in that place, that lonely, broken place, where God began to meet me. That was my *place called there*.

I wore masks and smiled when I wanted to cry. I faked strength in public but crumbled in private. I tried to "fit in" as a First Lady, attending church after church, conference after conference, traveling to convocations, always trying to keep it together. I loved ministry, but I desperately longed for balance. I wanted moments of laughter, rest, and renewal.

One day before he passed away, I asked my husband, "When are we going to take a vacation? When are we going to do something just for us, more than just church, home, and work?" We planned the trip, but he passed away before we ever got to take it. That type of pain and regret cuts deeper than most can imagine. Again, I know where my husband is spending eternity, but there was so much more that I wanted to experience with him while he was here on earth. We loved each other deeply and made the best of our 21 years together. After his passing, I entered a place that no one could help me navigate but God.

Loneliness, Healing, and the Process

The days after the funeral were the hardest. In the beginning, the phone calls poured in. Everyone wanted to check on me. But eventually, those calls slowed down. People returned to their lives, and I was left sitting in the quiet, alone in my house, in my *place called there.*

Yet even in that stillness, God showed up. He reminded me that He had never left me. That solitude became sacred. It was the place where God taught me to depend on Him for everything.

That season of isolation became a classroom of healing. God processed me there; not to punish me, but to prepare me. Sometimes the process is the tool He uses to develop our discipline, deepen our maturity, and teach us endurance. "There" won't look the same for everyone. It has no map, no instruction manual, no timeline. It often feels uncomfortable and unfair. But even when it doesn't feel good, it always works for our good.

The Woman Who Got There

As I close this chapter, I want to reflect on a woman who knew what suffering felt like, the woman with the issue of blood. Her story is found in **Mark 5:25–34**. She had been sick for twelve years, spending everything she had on doctors who couldn't heal her. She endured rejection, isolation, and disappointment. Yet, even in her suffering, she pressed forward.

She said within herself, *If I can just touch the hem of His garment, I will be made whole.* That was her *place called there*, the moment she decided to move past her pain and reach for Jesus. She was tired, but she was determined. She was desperate, but she was also full of faith.

Just like her, we have to press through the pain to reach that place called there. No matter what it looks like, no matter what others say, and no matter how broken we feel, we must keep reaching. Our ways are not God's ways, and our thoughts are not His thoughts. But whatever you do, make sure you get there, and while you're getting there, praise Him all the way.

Reader Journal Prompt

Take a few quiet moments to reflect on the questions below.

1. Think about a season in your life that felt like your own "place called there." What did God teach you about yourself and about His faithfulness during that time?

_____

_____

_____

_____

2. How has pain or loss shaped your spiritual maturity? What has the process produced in you that comfort and ease could not?

_____

_____

_____

_____

3. The woman with the issue of blood said, "If I can just get to Jesus." What does getting "there" look like for you today? What steps can you take to move closer to Him in faith?

_____

_____

_____

_____

Remember: The place called there may feel lonely, but it's never empty. God meets us there, molds us there, and strengthens us there until we rise whole again.

Mechelle Nenette Hayes

Born the first of four daughters of Bishop Robert & Evangelist Modena McPhee...sister of Yvette, Moleka & Robyn...wife and assistant to Senior Pastor E.W Hayes of Grace Ministries of Deliverance in Winston Salem, NC. Mentored by Dr. Ruth E. Creps-Crockett of Miami, Florida, where working under her leadership for 21 years was a blessing. I hold a Bachelor's & Master's Degree in Healthcare Administration with a specialty in Gerontology. Presently, I am employed at a Senior Assisted Living Community in Winston-Salem, North Carolina.

More Importantly,

- I am enthused about the things of God.
- A Worshipper...
- A Praiser...
- I love people & nothing matters to me like seeing lives impacted and encouraged by our "BIG GOD"... yet, in Christ I lack nothing. It is my desire to see people live sweat-less and victorious in Christ. I love what I do.. and do what I love... It is from this platform that I minister.

My theme song this year... "We serve a very big God who is always on my side".

Loving God!... loving life!... loving music!

80

Chapter 9

Sweatless Victories!

Pastor Mechelle Hayes

For I know the thoughts that I think toward you, saith the Lord, thoughts of peace, and not of evil, to give you an expected end. **-Jeremiah 29:11 KJV**

And we know [with great confidence] that God [who is deeply concerned about us] causes all things to work together [as a plan] for good for those who love God, to those who are called according to His plan and purpose. **-Romans 8:28 (AMP)**

I want to share a dream that greatly impacted my life. In this dream, I rescued a crying child who was stuck inside of my vehicle. I vividly recall that even though the child's legs were stuck temporarily, when the child asked, "How are you?" The child exclaimed, "I AM OK!!!"

"We've flown free from their fangs, free of their traps, free as a bird. Their grip is broken; we're free as a bird in flight."
-Psalms 124:7 (MSG)

There were rough times in my life that I almost gave up...I almost let go. But I give thanks, praises and ALL the glory to my Heavenly Father who, always causes us to triumph...GO JEHOVAH!!!!!!!!! Like the child in my dream, I praise the Lord that I am free and I am OK!!!

My mentor & Pastor Dr. "Mother Ruth E. Creps-Crockett many times, in the midst of challenging situations, gave voice to this statement and I echo it in this writing, "I MAY NOT FIT HERE BUT, I BELONG HERE!!! Presently, I have called three places home and have lived in each city for at least 16 years. Just like the baby whose legs were stuck in my vehicle said, "I'm ok", I am expressing today that I have experienced and will continue to experience Sweatless Victories, which is now my declaration & life's pursuit. With this in mind…nothing matters to me like seeing lives encouraged, impacted and changed by the power of God who affords us the ability of change through fulfillment of purpose a life. My prayer is that as you read this chapter, you will feel encouraged to confess you too are "OK" and that you will declare "Sweatless Victories" in every area of your life. Let's dive in.

What has made a difference in my life:

The way I speak has changed.

Words I spoke in the past resulted in many difficulties. Even though spoken innocently and in ignorance, those negative words still had a negative effect on my life. The bible teaches us that life and death is in the power of the tongue, so my ignorance did not negate the power of my words. On the other hand, since knowing and finding truth in the word of God, I have watched my life unfold beautifully because I chose to only speak the word of God over my life. Words are powerful!! The working of this statement has unfolded miracles, signs, and wonders in my life. I am committed to continuing in this vein so that I will always advance forward with remarkable success.

Now, when I experience difficult or challenging situations, I am careful with my response. I watch the words that come out of my mouth because I understand how powerful my words are. I am striving daily to become more skillful in how I speak and respond to situations, thereby creating a greater work, home, family and ministry experience. Through this intentional practice, my whole being is evolving as designed by my Heavenly Father. God and my obedience to His word is making me unstoppable physically, spiritually, emotionally, and financially. Now, with absolute certainty, I can confess, "The sky is the limit."

One of the prayer points that I have adopted from our storming the gates of a brand-new day session is "I choose life… I choose good… I choose God. Therefore…It is already mine! Jesus has already paid the price for it, and I want it…I want it ALLLL!!!!

The way I think has changed.

Finally, brothers and sisters, whatever is true, whatever is noble, whatever is right, whatever is pure, whatever is lovely, whatever is admirable—if anything is excellent or praiseworthy—think about such things. ⁹ Whatever you have learned or received or heard from me, or seen in me—put it into practice. And the God of peace will be with you.
-Philippians 4:8-9 (NIV)

The revealing of this truth and now the practice of it in my life is bringing forth God's desired results in my life.

For as far back as I can remember I was passive. The enemy had me believing that passivity was meekness. Let me be clear, the two are not the same! In my young adult life, I was very passive. I allowed anything not only to enter my mind, but I meditated on it and allowed what I meditated on to become reality. When I changed that practice and began meditating on the word of God and spending time in the presence of the Lord, I was introduced to a great wealth of Truth.

Now, I do not allow things that I hear or see to interfere with the truth of God's word. I have learned how to filter those things through to the word of God. I present them all to Him and what comes back from Him is what I hold on to and they become my truth. And though I have seen great results in my life, I know there is more. There is so much more for me.

When I did not know any better, passivity and feelings of despondency almost had the best of me, but because of the refreshing of the Lord, I now know there is more. I'm sensing there is more. I am seeing through the eyes of our Father that there is more. There is more hope, peace, life, and joy from God.

Because I have learned to live by Philippians 4:8-9, every time I travel, even if it is just taking short drives to the mountains,

I always receive enlightenment, encouragement and empowerment that results in answers to questions and concerns of my heart. I call it the mental reset!!! Spending time thinking and meditating on what God has instructed me to think about allows my mind to reset and refocus on the marvelous things He is doing in my life, family, and ministry!

There is more.

The Lord through His word has shown me that there is more!!! Spending time in His presence results in times of Sweatless Victories. This is what I desire, more sweatless victories in every area of my life. Therefore, I must continue to pass the challenge of thought processes, words others have spoken, and unspoken suggestions that could cause multiple manifestations. Right thinking and right speaking canceled out the things that I did not want in my life. Because I know there is more manifestation of God's promises in store for my life, I practice right thinking and right speaking more. The more I spend time listening to Him and soaking in His presence, the more I see "the more" He has prepared for me!

Note: If one were to stand on a high rise above a parade, you would be able to see the beginning, the middle, and the end. You would also be able to see any distractions that are present. I believe this same scenario is true in a life...my life. God knows all. God sees the beginning and end of every situation. With that in mind, following His prompting always gives the correct course to take and leads to a life filled with Sweatless Victories!!!!

Reader Journal Prompt

Take a few quiet moments to reflect on the questions below.

1. Think of a time when you felt trapped by life's circumstances but later realized that God was working behind the scenes. How did your perspective shift when you chose to speak life instead of defeat?

_____

_____

_____

_____

2. Reflect on Philippians 4:8–9. What thoughts or words have you allowed to shape your reality that no longer align with God's truth? What declarations can you begin speaking daily to align your mind and words with His promises?

_____

_____

_____

_____

3. What does a "Sweatless Victory" look like in your life right now? In what areas do you need to release control and trust God to do the heavy lifting?

_____

_____

_____

_____

Remember: Freedom begins with your words and is sustained by your thoughts. Speak life, think truth, and watch God turn your faith into sweatless victories.

Lauren Thomas is the Executive Pastor and First Lady at Victory in Christ Cathedral located in Brooklyn, New York.

Lady Thomas serves with vision, compassion, and a deep commitment to spiritual growth and community impact. A devoted wife of 19 years to Bishop Charles E. Thomas II and proud mother of two daughters, Charlotte and Zara, Lauren brings a nurturing spirit to every aspect of her life.

In addition to her pastoral work, Lauren is a licensed cosmetologist and the CEO of **Robin's Hair & Beauty**, a thriving business specializing in natural hair care and custom wig making. With a creative eye and a heart for empowering others, she has built a brand that celebrates beauty, confidence, and self-expression.

Lauren is especially passionate about mentoring youth and young adults, guiding them to discover their purpose and walk boldly in their faith. Whether in the pulpit, the salon, or the community, she is dedicated to uplifting others and making a lasting impact.

Chapter 10

Tag! You're It.

Lady Lauren Thomas

Do you remember playing tag as a child? Running for your life hoping that nobody caught you. Hoping that you wouldn't hear those dreaded words "Tag, you're it!". While most of the neighborhood kids loved playing this game, I sincerely loathed it. Whenever I'd play, I always got singled out, chased, and tagged within seconds. While I was "it", it seemed as though everyone I was chasing was faster, bigger, and better than I was. It usually ended with me walking away sweaty, tired, and upset. In a scenario like this, I could just walk away from the game and decide not to play. But what could I do when it felt like God was the one constantly "tagging" me in. Where do you run when your opponent is God?

I was born and raised in church. The daughter of an Assistant Pastor and Sunday school teacher, I was surrounded by love and community. My church family was all I knew. Missing a Sunday was not an option. If you were a church kid like me, you remember being in church all day on Sunday was not for the weak. My father was responsible for opening the church doors every Sunday and teaching the adult Sunday school class while my mother taught the children's class. Service began right after that at 11:30 and then there was a break.

During this break, the saints would go home, eat, take a nap, and come back to church for the 6:30pm service! Some families would invite others to their homes to eat together and some would even bring dinner to the church and take a nap there. Afterwards, the real fellowship would begin where the children would play, and the women would talk. The men would laugh and debate everything from the scriptures to sports. This would go on until someone realized they had to get up in the morning and then the hour-long goodbyes would begin. This was my life; this was my family. Perfectly imperfect and carefree until one day I got tagged and I didn't even know I was in the game.

At six years old the rug was pulled from under me, and everything changed. My mother died. She was gone and nothing would ever be the same again. Her death was the hit on my back that came without warning and far too soon. I grew up very quickly as a result. My little sister was just 8 months old when she left us, and I became her protector and second mother. My Grandmother moved in, and my Godparents stepped up to help. My church family was front and center making sure my father, younger sister and I were cared for.

Although there was all this love surrounding me, I still felt completely abandoned, alone, unwanted, and unprotected.

90

The devil magnified these feelings to drag me down a course that could have ended so many ways. He may have wanted to take me out, but the voice of God kept saying "You're It".

When God has a call on your life, you can bet the enemy is going to come with everything he has to throw you off course. He tries to recreate who God made you to be, to fit your environment and circumstances. God may have created you to be soft, nurturing, and ambitious, but instead you become hard, careless, and lethargic. He wants to be God so bad! I'm so glad the one true and living God is faithful even when we aren't. When we can't see how things can be any different or how we could ever change, He remains committed to the process of bringing us into purpose. Life will teach you that God is more committed to us than we are to Him. I learned this firsthand during my seasons of running away from God.

Trying to run away from an all-seeing, all-knowing, ever-present God is crazy work. Where can you go, except places you have convinced yourself that God is not present. When I was just 13 years old, I had a profound moment with God where He used a friend of mine to show me Psalms 27 very randomly one day. We were teen girls who never talked Bible, but this day we did. While reading this chapter with her, Verse 10 really stood out and spoke very loudly to me. "Even if my father and mother abandon me, the Lord will hold me close." (Ps. 27:10 NLT) This biblical promise cut through the mental anguish and let me know that He had me. With all the darkness I felt inside; after reading that verse, my heart was filled with so much light and love. I finally felt like somebody was looking after me and loved me for real. However, whatever God was doing on the inside, was up against a battle with peer-pressure and hormones which were waiting for me on the outside.

At this point, my father had already remarried and was going through a divorce. So, not only was my world being shaped by death but also by divorce. I was shown in more ways than one that I was an unwanted inconvenience, so I started running. I ran looking for spaces to hide among the weeds hoping that no one would see the "real" me. My friends wanted me to be around, and more importantly BOYS wanted me around. These boys had a way of making everything you said and did, seem like gold pouring out of a beautiful fountain. All they did was take advantage of a broken mind and wounded heart. I was lured into a place of false security, knowing fully that I did not belong there either.

By 18 years old, I was homeless and living anywhere I could. From couch to couch at friends' homes or wherever someone would let me in. Working, partying, drinking, and sleeping around was my open rebellion to my parents as well as God. Although this was my weekly habit, I still made sure I was in church every Sunday. I would sit in the back of the church with my blonde hair and tight dresses, but I was still there. I'm not sure if it was guilt that brought me there or my acute awareness that God was chasing me.

It appeared all my peers where able to do whatever they wanted to do without any internal conflict or concern, but I would immediately feel the chastising hand of God resting on every bad decision I made. At work one day a woman that I'd never met before came to me crying. I'll never forget what she said to me that day. Through her tears she said, 'You have no idea how important you are to God. Please, please do what He says.' All I could say was "okay", but I knew that was not something that happened to everyone. I also knew I had no real intention of honoring that request. I was having too much "fun" being silly and blind.

On another occasion I went to a club with a group of friends, and I was already tipsy upon arrival. We were dancing the night away and having so much fun when out of nowhere a girl standing right next to me got stabbed. She was so close I had her blood on my pants. Yet again, I knew that was God and still kept running.

Another time, I went to meet up with a guy and was almost raped. I tried to get him off me and said no many times to no avail. I saw his face distort to where I knew this was a demonic attack on my life. Seeing his face caused me to stop talking to him and turn my plea towards God. I said to God I am sorry: if you get me out of this, I will serve you and I whispered the name, Jesus. As quickly as his face changed, is as quickly as it returned to normal. He got off me and said to me, "You better go home." I ran out so fast and thanked God the whole way home.

These experiences, and more, forced me to come to terms with the fact that I could not run faster than God and all I was doing was making a big mess. I was playing with fire, and I was on my way to getting burned. For some reason He singled me out and was bigger than me. Eventually, He was going to win.

Some people are allowed to run and hide for years doing whatever they want to do. Some people search for peace with things that only bring more torment and disaster and are never able to truly come back from it. No matter how long it takes you to stop running, or what it takes for you to stop, be grateful for the mercy and grace that kept you on this side of heaven. Be grateful for the opportunity to allow Him to change you and make you His own. For me it took a lot of hard knocks, but within a very short window of time. I often say God had me on a short leash because He knew the enemy wanted to destroy my entire life. God had work for me to do but first He had work to do in me.

Running from God is a waste of time and energy, especially since we have no idea how much time we have left here. Once I yielded, my life changed drastically in a year. I got married, bought a home, got a stable job, and became First Lady of the same church I was born in within three years. The enemy tried his best to make me believe the lie that said I was alone and unwanted. Once I was no longer blind and defensive, I could see the truth so clearly. I was never alone at any point, and neither are you. Even while I was running there were many people who loved me and were praying for me. God decided to show me just how much He loved me by giving me a husband who is the perfect example of how Christ loves the church. I was messy, confused and broken but he would give absolutely anything just to be with me. I still struggle with the thought of being loved so deeply and completely by not just a physical man, but also a Holy and perfect God.

My passion for years has been for the youth of this generation because they often are misunderstood and unseen. Young people in each generation are always the enemy's target but are largely unprotected and left vulnerable by adults who are dealing with their own demons from when they themselves were young and unprotected.

If you're reading this and you're trying not to get 'tagged', let me tell you firsthand it's easier to just surrender. Give up and know that you aren't losing anything but instead you are gaining everything. God created you with purpose and He is the only one with the manual on how to use you. You are too important to God.

Too much power is given to people who are flesh and blood just like you and are capable of mistakes, just like you. Not one person can claim perfection because as long as we are alive, there is always room for change and growth. However, there is a perfect God who never changes because there is no need for Him to change; He is Perfect. He will never let you down. There are times where it seems like He's the biggest let down ever and you are a fool for trusting Him. I can confidently tell you that on the other side of those hard days, the goodness of God is waiting for you.

Romans 8:28 (KJV) says that *"…all things work together for good to them that love God, to them who are the called according to His purpose."* That means even your bad days are on assignment to bless you somehow. When it feels like you're falling to pieces and holding on by a thread, remember that as tightly as you believe you are holding on to God, He's holding on to you even tighter. You may find yourself asking 'Why me?' as those feelings of worthlessness and insecurity flood in. You may think you've done too much wrong and have gone too far outside of the will of God, but before you go down that road, take an assessment of who is talking. The devil fills our head with lies that are contrary to what God has always said. He's been using that same tactic since the beginning. However, you were never out of God's reach, so you are never too far. Ever since the garden, it was always you that He was after. His arms are not too short to save; He's just waiting on your surrender.

I still don't like playing Tag and probably never will. When it comes to God though, I see that He was never my opponent, He was my prize. Once I realized that, 'Tag, you're it' was never something I needed to run from because what it really meant was 'Tag, You're Mine!'

Reader Journal Prompt

Take a few quiet moments to reflect on the questions below.

1. Reflect on a time when you tried to "run" from God's call or
   His correction. What finally caused you to stop running, and
   how did your life change once you surrendered?

   _____

   _____

   _____

   _____

2. When have you experienced the closeness of God in a season
   of loss, rejection, or loneliness? How did that awareness of His
   presence reshape your understanding of love and belonging?

   _____

   _____

   _____

   _____

3. What does it mean to you personally to be "God's"? How does
   that truth challenge or encourage the way you see yourself and
   live out your purpose today?

   _____

   _____

   _____

   _____

Remember: God isn't chasing you to punish you. He's pursuing
you to remind you that you've always belonged to Him.

Lady Penny Hauser is a truly inspirational witness to how her faith, leadership, and unwavering devotion enriches both her family life and her Jehovah Nissi church family's life every day.

As a mantle holder of this vital role, she beautifully continues the legacy that she and her late husband, Bishop Larry Clinton Hauser Sr., lovingly established within the congregation and beyond. Her deep commitment to the spiritual guidance for the church community, alongside her wonderful experience as a mother to Lisa, Jacqueline, and Larry Jr., clearly demonstrates her strength and dedication in all aspects of life.

Her professional journey, which includes over two decades as a manager at Rent A Center (R.A.C.) and her education from Louisburg Junior College and UNC Charlotte, underscores her remarkable resilience and her leadership qualities, which empower those around her in both professional and personal spheres. Penny's cherished scripture, John 3:16, beautifully reflects her profound faith in God's boundless love and enduring grace, a guiding principle evident in her actions and interactions.

Acknowledgments

My four extraordinary women who have shaped my life, each leaving an imprint in my heart.

- **Mary Strong, the pillar of resilience**—She taught me that true strength lies in faith and resourcefulness. Her wisdom showed me how to trust that God can multiply even the smallest blessings.

- **Joyce Wilson, the heart of love**—She embodied kindness and compassion, proving that everyone deserves love, regardless of who they are. Her example inspired me to embrace others wholeheartedly.

- **Pastor Jacqueline Ingram, the champion of excellence**—My mother instilled in me the value of integrity and determination. She made it clear that anything worth doing is worth doing well, pushing me to pursue my goals with purpose and diligence.

- **Elect Lady Juliette Robinson, the keeper of tradition and faith**—As our matriarch, she carries the torch of wisdom, reminding us that faith is the foundation of our unity. Her devotion strengthens our family and keeps us anchored in God's presence.

Together, their teachings have shaped my resilience, compassion, discipline, and faith, values that continue to guide me. Their collective wisdom has reinforced four essential truths:

- **Faith and trust in God**—They have all taught me to rely on His wisdom, provision, and unwavering presence.

- **Strength and resilience**—Through faith, love, and discipline, they showed me how to overcome challenges with grace.

- **Love and compassion**—Joyce's belief in unconditional love is reflected in each woman's wisdom, proving that kindness unites us all.

- **Commitment to excellence**—Jacqueline's insistence on doing things the right way, paired with Juliette's devotion to family, instilled in me the value of dedication and responsibility.

These women have molded me into the person I am today, and their impact continues to inspire those around me.

Lisa, Jacqueline, and Larry Hauser, you are the sources of my strength, resilience, and love. You are the three forces that keep me moving forward, and your impact on my life is immeasurable. I honor and acknowledge you for your unwavering dedication, commitment, and love to me.

To those who have been there to catch my tears, delight in my joy, and encourage me through the rough moments...God loves you, and so do I. No matter how far we stretch, we will always find our way back as long as we never break.

To the love of my life, the late Bishop Larry Clinton Hauser, we pushed our limits but never wavered. I will love you always.

#TeamHauser

Chapter 11

A Ruby in God's Hands: Embracing the Role of First Lady

Lady Penny Hauser

"But they that wait upon the LORD shall renew their strength; they shall mount up with wings as eagles; they shall run, and not be weary; and they shall walk, and not faint." **-Isaiah 40:31**

The Life of a Pastor's Wife

"She is clothed with strength and dignity; she can laugh at the days to come." **-Proverbs 31:25**

A pastor's wife faces a lot more than just sitting on the front row and looking pretty. The responsibilities and challenges are immense. My grandmother's advice about needing both a Bible and a baseball bat is poignant; it highlights the need to be spiritually strong but also ready to defend and support those around you. Being misled, I thought everything would be easy as a pastor's wife, boy was I led astray. It was eye-opening when I realized that people would smile at you on Sunday and stab you in the back on Wednesday." That is when I learn to look to the hills which comes my help, my help comes from the Lord. In this role as a pastor's wife, I understood you have to be Ford tough.

Juggling Roles and Responsibilities

"I can do all this through him who gives me strength." -**Philippians 4:13**

As a First Lady, I juggled many roles—organizing programs, stepping in when others did not, cleaning the church, praying for people, listening to their problems, taking care of my family and neglecting myself to ensure everything ran smoothly. Bishop's words about punctuality always emphasized the importance of being diligent and timely. You encounter numerous challenges and see the true nature of people when punctuality is not demonstrated. Many people want to shine but are unwilling to do the work required.

The Value of True Friends

"A friend loves at all times, and a brother is born for a time of adversity." -**Proverbs 17:17**

Throughout my hard times, I had several people who supported and encouraged me. True friends are those you can count on one hand. Some people loved me for who I was, while others saw it as a way to gain prestige and power. True friends are those who stand by you during the midnight hours of tears or at a restaurant where you can cry for hours without fear of judgment or gossip. They don't ask for anything in return; they simply say, 'Whatever you need, I got you.' These friends are different from those who ask for favors or money or stay at your house while blaming you for their problems or for not being available when they wanted you to.

Real friends are hard to come by, but they are the ones who stand by you through thick and thin, without seeking recognition or rewards. True friends will be there for you in your darkest hours, providing support and comfort without expecting anything in return.

When people come into your life, some come for a season to help you share, grow, or learn. Some may show you how to turn away and run, but others will bring you an experience of peace or make you laugh. They may teach you something you have never done, and these are the ones who will stay for a lifetime. They usually give you an unbelievable amount of joy.

Feeling Lost and Unworthy

"For the Spirit God gave us does not make us timid, but gives us power, love and self-discipline." **-2 Timothy 1:7**

It's funny how we know that God does not give us a spirit of fear but a spirit of a sound mind. Yet, what do you do when you feel lost? What do you do when you feel like you've lost your voice, and embarrassment makes you want to hide? You feel invisible, sitting in the back row at church, hoping nobody recognizes you. Despite this, they still call you to be the lady with the pastor. How can you be worthy of that title when you have felt like the least for so long? This is genuinely how I felt: everyone looking at me, judging me, making me feel unworthy of leading people. When Jehovah Nissi closed her doors, my world came tumbling down. I felt as though God had left me and everyone who said they would be there left too. I wanted to crawl under a rock, but God.

God's Humor and Encouragement

"So do not fear, for I am with you; do not be dismayed, for I am your God. I will strengthen you and help you; I will uphold you with my righteous right hand." **-Isaiah 41:10**

God, in His great sense of humor, still sends people to me, seeking words of encouragement even as I try to be invisible. Today, I received a call at work from a customer who shared personal struggles and downfalls, letting me know that my words of encouragement were what they needed to keep going. My job involves interacting with customers from all facets of life who often share their struggles, seeking encouragement and prayer. Even when I feel like I'm bleeding internally, they keep coming. It's as if God is saying, 'You were designed not to be in the back but to be in the front. You're supposed to shine like a ruby, forged with heat and pressure, to be what I designed you to be.'

What I've gone through has allowed me to be transparent, helping others understand that being the least doesn't mean being the worst; it makes you humble and appreciative of God's blessings.

Reflecting on Ministry While Discovering My Calling

"Therefore, my dear brothers and sisters, stand firm. Let nothing move you. Always give yourselves fully to the work of the Lord, because you know that your labor in the Lord is not in vain." **-1 Corinthians 15:58**

"For I know the plans I have for you," declares the Lord, "plans to prosper you and not to harm you, plans to give you hope and a future." **-Jeremiah 29:11**

As I look back over the five years in ministry, I realize that learning what to do and what not to do was my portion. As a First Lady, I thought my calling was just to support my husband, encourage him, and stay in the background. But God had a call on my life too. People would call me 'pastor,' and I would insist that I wasn't because I hadn't been ordained. However, whether ordained or not, if God has instilled that calling in you, it remains. Just because you lack the title doesn't mean you don't have the call. God wants you to obey and do what He says because you're holding others up until you reach your full potential. Everyone has people assigned to them, and you can't do the Lord's full work until you know who you are and your place in the Kingdom.

Supporting the Pastor

"Two are better than one, because they have a good return for their labor: If either of them falls down, one can help the other up. But pity anyone who falls and has no one to help them up." **-Ecclesiastes 4:9-10**

The role of a pastor's wife is much more than it appears on the surface. It's about being there for your husband, supporting him, and covering him in prayer. People often don't see the struggles and sacrifices that come with the role of a pastor's wife. They put pastors and their families on pedestals, not realizing they are human too, facing their own battles. There were moments when the Bishop and I, along with our children, would be out doing family events, and just like that, the phone would ring. Larry, both husband and dad, now becomes the Bishop, torn away from his family because people did not heed the Word preached and expected him to solve all of their problems. This, in turn, caused problems for his own family. Many ignored the man and only saw him as the pastor of the church. They did not understand that he had a job, friends, and family, but most importantly, he needed to spend time with the Lord.

Overcoming Heaviness

"The Lord is close to the brokenhearted and saves those who are crushed in spirit." **-Psalm 34:18**

Unfortunately, Larry, my husband, became very discouraged, oppressed, and weighted down with the cares of the world.

Carrying the burdens of others, when he needed those who depended on him to lift him up in prayer and come to just check on him, none were to be found. After my husband's passing, the heaviness held me back from my purpose. This chapter is for the woman who feels she can't make it, who thinks she needs a man to validate her worth. It's for the woman to know that God can rebuild, heal, strengthen, and awaken her in ways she couldn't before. Despite everything, I can stand because of God's ultimate love. This walk is individual, sad, happy, and joyful, but it's a walk only you can walk out, and it is not for the faint at heart.

God's Glory Shines Through

"And we know that in all things God works for the good of those who love him, who have been called according to his purpose." -**Romans 8:28**

Despite the criticism and laughter of others, God's glory shines through. He still blesses, restores, and heals. Even through the embarrassment of people talking about my husband, God restored him, changed his life, and elevated him. My husband took his last breath knowing that God is still God, and He makes no mistakes.

Embracing the Journey of Faith

"Not only so, but we also glory in our sufferings, because we know that suffering produces perseverance; perseverance, character; and character, hope. And hope does not put us to shame, because God's love has been

poured out into our hearts through the Holy Spirit, who has been given to us." -**Romans 5:3-5**

The journey of a pastor's wife is filled with challenges and responsibilities that go far beyond the surface. It requires spiritual strength, unwavering support, and a heart ready to serve others. Through the ups and downs, the moments of feeling lost and unworthy, and the times when God's sense of humor brings unexpected opportunities to encourage others, you have discovered the true essence of your calling.

God's divine plan and purpose shine through the trials and tribulations, teaching valuable lessons about humility, resilience, and the importance of knowing who you are in Him. The journey has revealed the significance of true friends, the power of prayer, and the transformative process that shapes you into the person God designed you to be.

Ultimately, my story is a testament to God's unwavering love, His ability to rebuild and heal, in the strength that comes from embracing my calling. As I walk this path, I continue to inspire and uplift others, demonstrating that even in the face of adversity, God's glory shines through like a ruby, restoring and elevating those who remain faithful to His purpose.

Reader Journal Prompt

Take a few quiet moments to reflect on the questions below.

1. Reflect on a season when you carried a heavy load while still showing up for others. How did God sustain you when no one else seemed to notice your struggle?

    _____

    _____

    _____

    _____

2. Think about a difficult moment in your life that taught you something about your purpose. How did that season help refine your character, deepen your faith, or clarify your calling?

    _____

    _____

    _____

    _____

3. Where are you still seeking validation from others instead of resting in who God says you are? What practical steps can you take to embrace your divine identity and walk confidently in your own calling?

    _____

    _____

    _____

    _____

Remember: The fire that refines you does not destroy you, it reveals the ruby God has placed within you.

Lady Michlin Bailey is the radiant First Lady of One Word Fellowship Worship Center in Winston-Salem, NC, where she serves faithfully alongside her husband of 28 years, Bishop John S. Bailey, II. Living out Psalm 118:24, "This is the day which the Lord hath made; we will rejoice and be glad in it," she embraces each day with grace, joy, and purpose. A devoted wife, mother, grandmother, and mentor, she embodies the strength and poise of a Proverbs 31 woman.

With over 25 years in healthcare and a heart for ministry, Lady Bailey previously led the Fine Arts Ministry at Fresh Fire Worship Center before accepting the call to evangelism in 2017. She later founded The Women's Filling Station, One Word's women's ministry, empowering countless women in their walk with Christ. Known for her warm spirit and hands-on leadership, she serves wherever needed and treasures time with her husband, children (John III & Michjohnna), and granddaughter Milayah all while walking boldly in God's favor.

A funny story as a First Lady…

As a First Lady, I am my husband's biggest amen corner, and if you're honest, you are too! Not some of the time, but *all the time* we are the amen corner. They're going to shift their head toward us 99 times every sermon. Have you ever felt like your head was going to fall off of your shoulders, because you've bounced back and forth so much to let your man know you have his back, his front, and his side? Or have you felt tingly feelings in your hands as if they're going to fall off, because you've clapped, plunged, and waved so many times as he is preaching? As I am writing this down, it makes me chuckle. I am sure a lot of you can agree that this still holds true to this day. I know this is an inside joke that only pastors' wives will understand but it's okay to laugh because we all know it's true! So… go ahead and get your laughter on!

"This is the day the LORD has made; We will rejoice and be glad in it."- **Psalms 118:24**

Chapter 12

The Gift

Lady Michlin Bailey

"Likewise the Spirit also helpeth our infirmities: for we know not what we should pray for as we ought: but the Spirit itself maketh intercession for us with groanings which cannot be uttered." -
Romans 8:26 KJV

A s I begin, I am comforted in knowing that we have help along this Christian journey! When I was asked to be a part of this blessed anthology, which I am humbled and honored to join, I began to consult with the Holy Spirit who is the Third Person of the Trinity, the Teacher of the church, the Convictor of the church, our Advocate, and the Paraclete, "called to one's side." I was compelled to share about the Gift by mention of the Holy Spirit. I will share more later on the One who is called to one's side!

I felt a quickening in my spirit right then! Oh wow! Did you feel your spirit connect with the thought of that...the Help being called to your side? If not, it will before this chapter is over.

As we explore the depth of who He is (the Gift, the Help), I feel certain that reassured strength will catapult you deeper into your next level in God. Like a breath of fresh air, a renewed mindset to walk out your God truth, that hope, future, and expected end God declares in Jeremiah 29:11. I hear expansion in the Spirit! When we truly know how to walk in tandem with the Holy Spirit, our life shifts upward in ways we never deemed possible. Listen woman, listen my sister, and I voice this with power from our Lord and Savior Jesus Christ, who is the same yesterday, today, and forevermore, YOU are not alone!

Now, I have experienced the Gift to be a very present help in the time of trouble, and well, that's His good job. Good meaning purposeful, attentive, on guard, and sure-footed. Jesus Christ talks extensively about the Gift and His good job. John 16:13 states, "But when He, the Spirit of truth, comes, He will guide you into all truth." His good job.

Peter also speaks of the Gift. In the book of Acts, Peter speaks about the Holy Spirit being poured out on believers at Pentecost, enabling them to speak in different languages. His good job. This passage of Scripture corresponds with the Scripture that Jesus spoke to the disciples. He gave instruction to them by expressing that He had to go to prepare a place for them, but He would send back His Spirit. The Apostle Paul writes, "May the God of hope fill you with all joy and peace in believing, so that by the power of the Holy Spirit you may abound in hope." (Romans 15:13) And we know that all Scripture is God-breathed!

As we travel a little further through Scripture, it states, and I like how it reads in the ERV, "I will ask the Father, and He will give you another Helper to be with you forever." (John 14:16) Oh God, I thank You! It's the divine strategy for   me. His selfless act yielded His yes concerning us. In the passage above, Jesus was talking to His disciples to ease their concern about His departure. He gives voice to, "I have to go and prepare a place for you," but don't give up, don't get weary in well-doing, don't throw in the towel. Meaning the story is not over! My God, my God! I will give you HELP, the Holy Spirit! A present help in trouble.

It reminds me of the song, "Well, He walks with me, and He talks with me, and tells me I am His own!" This holds so much weight in my heart today. I can hear Him saying, "Don't go that way, my daughter. Read this Scripture for your brokenness: 'He heals the brokenhearted and binds up their wounds.'" (Psalm 147:3) I can hear Him saying, "Come here. I'll be that peace (Jehovah Shalom) that surpasses all understanding, that will guard your heart and mind through Christ Jesus. Shun evil, meaning stay away from evil at all costs. The Holy Spirit is upholding you in prayer through intercession because you don't always know how and what to pray for as you ought. I, the Holy Spirit, will be your comforter and guide."

In essence, don't lean on your own understanding because your understanding is flawed, and the Holy Spirit, the Gift, the Help, knows the perfect will of the Father. We've already stated that they are one. He can't operate against Himself. The Bible says, "For I know the thoughts and plans I think toward you, saith the Lord, thoughts of peace and not of evil," another version states, "to give a hope and a future, to give you an expected end." (Jeremiah 29:11) Are you regaining your strength for the journey? Do you feel that present help in times of trouble? Selah!

Selah means to burst forth with praise, sing loud of His goodness, to lift Him up and exalt His holy and matchless name! If you are feeling strength, and I believe you are because of the Help, because of the GIFT, then use those muscles and those nerves controlled by the nervous system in your mouth and have yourself a SELAH moment!

I'll never forget the time my baby well, she's a grown woman now, but at the time she was six years old, became very unwell. We learned she had appendicitis, which caused her appendix to rupture and created spores around the abdominal wall. This was a life-threatening emergency, so she immediately had to have surgery. Before it all unfolded, the Holy Spirit came to me in a dream. I remember it so clearly. There was a fire, which represented trouble in the dream. I remember His hand; it was beautiful too, a crystal-clear vision of His hand coming toward me, nudging me to wake up, be on post, be alert, be vigilant because there's trouble in the land.

Not many days after my dream, my daughter became very ill! He was a very present HELP in our time of trouble. This is one of many occasions He, the Holy Spirit, the Gift showed up and showed out on my behalf! If it had not been for the Lord who was on my side! Selah!

Ladies, and I'll include the gentlemen as well, just in case they're partaking in reading this chapter (lol), we have Help! He is sweet, I know! The GIFT is the third Person of the Trinity, who has feelings. He is all God and all Deity. He is the Ruach of God, which denotes the very breath, spirit, and life of God! God the Son is He, He is them, and they are one! 1 John 5:7 KJV gives lens to what I'm writing: "For there are three that bear record in heaven, the Father, the Word (Jesus), and the Holy Ghost: and these three are one."

As you walk through this chapter, my prayer is this: that your relationship with the Holy Spirit will become relevant in your everyday life! In telling the story of who He is and how essential He is in my life, I pray doors will open that no man can close, and close doors that were meant to harm you, in Jesus Christ's name.

As believers, we must hold fast to our confession of hope without wavering, for He who promised is faithful (Hebrews 10:23). So, no matter what we face on a day-to-day basis, our God reigns supreme! If He said it, He is well able to perform it, and He honors His word above His name. In times past, I have really tunneled through the thick of some things, and the natural man will present a smokescreen that there's no way out, it's not going to change, this is where your situation will stay—but there's that word again! It takes me to a God place every time because there's more! God is not through yet! It hasn't all been revealed yet! I know He's able to do exceeding, abundantly, above all I can ask or think, according to the power that works within me! In the spirit, it's already done, and by faith, I say that it is so! Able God, You are! My sisters, ladies, He can handle it!

Paraclete- called to one's side! In my process of writing this chapter, I learned that the word Paraclete is the Greek meaning transferred into English, which means Comforter and Advocate. Publicly speaking, as a wife and First Lady, I can definitely announce that this statement holds true to this very day! I have seen Him at my side! Thank You, Jesus! To put it into perspective, He, the Holy Spirit, is constant. Constant, defined in Webster's Dictionary, means occurring continuously over a period of time. Constant, in the biblical sense, means the Holy Spirit's continuous presence and work within believers guiding, empowering, and sanctifying them. For me, there are two aspects to the Holy Spirit being Constant that I would like to mention. Thank you, Holy Spirit!

He's Constant, meaning He hears and knows everything. We already stated that He knows the perfect will of the Father. He's the third Person of the Trinity, co-equal and co-eternal with God the Father and Son. Even in knowing, sometimes my mouth or flesh tries to persuade me to say things concerning me that are not truth. Comments like, "You sure,

Holy Spirit?" or "God, was that You?" or things like, "You're not worthy to be a preacher," "You're not gifted enough to teach or write a chapter for an anthology." "Please, how are you going to help your husband reach his fullest potential, purpose, and goals?" I quickly learned that these are called empty conversations before the Lord. Yes, I said empty.

Jeremiah brought light to, "Before I formed you in the womb, I knew you; before you were born, I sanctified you; and I ordained you a prophet to the nations." "My frame was not hidden from you when I was being made in secret, intricately woven in the depths of the earth." God had a strategic plan for us all. Your makeup comes directly from the God who is more than enough, the One who is Omnipresent, Omnipotent, Omniscient, Omnibenevolent!

Have you ever had empty conversations with the Holy Spirit, the third Person of the Trinity? Have you ever tried to dispute with God over being a royal priesthood and a holy nation? I think we've all had moments, but the Gift by way of the Holy Spirit immediately brings the Word of God back to my remembrance. He brings back to my mind the Word of God because again, He honors His Word above His name! "I will praise You, O Lord, for I am fearfully and wonderfully made; marvelous are the works of Your hands." "I know the thoughts and plans I think toward you, saith the Lord." "Greater is He that's in you than he who is in the world." "What then shall we say to these things? If God be for you, who can be against you?" Sheesh! I began to feel myself getting stronger! Even now, hearing and confessing what the

Word of God says concerning my life quickens my spirit! In those moments, I feel my vigor, energy, radiance, and vitality come back stronger than ever because His Word is truth and every man a liar. His Word is our shield and our buckler! His Word is a lamp unto our feet and a light unto our path. Constant, the Gift, Help, called to one's side. God instructed me to share this in hopes that it would be life-changing for those who read it. As a result, it would serve as a push to keep going.

The second part of the twofold Constant One is the Fruit of the Spirit, which are the attributes and characteristics of the Holy Spirit, the Gift, against such there is no law: love, joy, peace, patience, kindness, goodness, faithfulness, gentleness, and self-control. If the Constant One lives on the inside of you, these fruits should always be at work in us.

That very present Help, the Gift, flows at the optimal level at all times because He is God. His movements are God, His thoughts are God, His ways are God, so He is well capable of achieving everything that God has willed for our lives. Scripture says, "God already knows our deepest thoughts, and He understands what the Spirit is saying because the Spirit speaks for His people in the way that agrees with what God wants." (Romans 8:27 ERV)

When I realized how essential the Holy Spirit is to our everyday walk and life, I think I had an epiphany! Our personal Intercessor… I began to study about Him, I began to call on Him! I wanted to understand everything about Him.

Intercessor: Helps believers pray, especially when they feel uncertain or overwhelmed.

Guide: One who helps people understand God, make decisions, and live holy lives.

Teacher of the Church: Gives understanding and direction on how to operate effectively through the Word of God, which will produce an effortless Zoe life.

Convictor: Reminds us that the wages of sin is death, but the gift of God is eternal life in Christ Jesus our Lord.

Comforter: The divine presence who provides solace, support, and peace to believers during times of hardship and distress, essentially acting as a source of comfort.

This is when I became a big girl in the spirit, and I'm yet still growing. As believers, we will ever be growing and learning. God is inexhaustible. He never runs out. There's no match to His greatness. I began to understand that He is key to living a true Zoe kind of life that God so desires us to have! He has been my greatest asset! We have been equipped with the best—God's Spirit—to help navigate our everyday life.

The Holy Spirit is a guarantee of God's promises. The Bible says, and this was good to me, "In Him, you also, when you heard the word of truth, the good news of your salvation, and as a result believed in Him, were stamped with the seal of the promised Holy Spirit [the One promised by Christ] as owned and protected by God. The Spirit is the guarantee [the first installment, the pledge, a foretaste] of our inheritance until the redemption of God's own possession [His believers], to the praise of His glory." (Ephesians 1:13–14 AMP)

Listen ladies, listen my sisters, listen Ecclesia—you have help! The Gift that keeps on giving, never sleeps nor slumbers, always watching over our souls. As I end my chapter, in the voice of my hubby and Bishop, "That's what the Lord told me to tell you today!" And after you have read it, I pray that going forward you will be able to say all day, "I've been with Jesus!" I love you all, and I mean it! May I leave you with this prayer:

Our father which art in heaven Hallowed be thy name. Thy kingdom come. Thy will be done on earth, as it is in heaven. And forgive us, our debts, as we forgive our debtors. And lead us not until temptation, but deliver us from evil: For thine is the kingdom, and the power, and the glory forever. Amen.

Oh, most wise Heavenly Father, I thank You for another opportunity to come before You in prayer. To approach Your throne of grace. There is none that would ever be able to supersede Your divine abilities! You reign supreme in all things! Thank you for the opportunity to be a part of this amazing Anthology. May the words of our mouth, and the mediation of our hearts be acceptable in your sight, for thine is the glory and the power forever and ever! May the minds and hearts of the reads catapult deeper and deeper in You in Jesus Christ name! May there be a reset of Your glory in their lives. May they know the Holy Spirit in depths they never had before, in Jesus name. May the readers of this chapter or Anthology understand line upon line and percept upon percept in Jesus Christ name I do pray. Amen and amen!

Reader Journal Prompt

Take a few quiet moments to reflect on the questions below.

1. Reflect on a time when you clearly sensed the Holy Spirit guiding, comforting, or warning you. How did that experience deepen your trust in God's presence?

    _____

    _____

    _____

    _____

2. What "empty conversations" have you had with God; moments when you questioned your worth or purpose? How can you replace those thoughts with the truth of His Word about who you are?

    _____

    _____

    _____

    _____

3. The Fruit of the Spirit: love, joy, peace, patience, kindness, goodness, faithfulness, gentleness, and self-control are signs of the Holy Spirit's constant work within us. Which of these fruits do you see growing in your life right now, and which one do you sense the Holy Spirit calling you to cultivate more intentionally?

    _____

    _____

    _____

    _____

Remember: The Holy Spirit is not distant or silent — He is your daily Helper, your constant Companion, and the very breath of God living within you.

Closing Prayer: A Prayer of Surrender and Strength

"Create in me a clean heart, O God, and renew a right spirit within me."
— Psalm 51:10 (KJV)

Heavenly Father,

Thank You for every word, every revelation, and every stirring of the heart that has taken place through this book. We stand in awe of Your goodness. Even in our weakness, You have been strong. Even in our uncertainty, You have been sure. And even in our silence, You have still been speaking.

Lord, we open our hearts to You once more.
Breathe on us, Holy Spirit.
Revive what has grown weary.
Reignite what has dimmed with time.
Restore what life has tried to take from us.
Let Your Spirit rush through the cracks of our souls like a fresh wind of grace.

We surrender every burden, every "why," every disappointment, and every delay.
We trust that nothing in our story is wasted in Your hands.
Turn our pain into power.
Turn our fear into faith.
Turn our weariness into worship.

Teach us to hear Your whisper above the noise.
Remind us that we are never alone — that the same Spirit who hovered over the waters in Genesis hovers over our lives even now.
Holy Spirit, be our constant companion, our comfort in chaos, our voice of truth, and our gentle guide through every unknown.

Father, let Your glory shine through us.
Let Your peace guard us.
Let Your love surround us.
And let Your Word take root so deeply that it produces a harvest of courage, confidence, and unwavering faith.

We close this book, but not this moment.
We close these pages, but not our pursuit of You.
Keep stirring, keep speaking, keep shaping us until our lives reflect Your heart in full.

We declare that the same power that raised Jesus from the dead lives within us.
Because of that truth, fear is defeated, faith is restored, and hope is reborn.

Thank You, Lord, for being the constant — our Helper, our Advocate, and our everlasting Friend.

In the mighty, matchless, and miracle-working name of Jesus Christ, amen.

Reflection:

Pause here. Close your eyes and breathe in the presence of God.

What parts of this book resonated most deeply within you? In the space below, write about how you feel God is calling you to move forward from here as you embrace the rest of your life with grace.

_____
_____
_____
_____
_____
_____
_____
_____
_____
_____
_____
_____
_____
_____
_____
_____
_____
_____
_____
_____
_____

"Now unto Him that is able to keep you from falling, and to present you faultless before the presence of His glory with exceeding joy, to the only wise God our Savior, be glory and majesty, dominion and power, both now and forever. Amen. **-Jude 1:24-25 (KJV)**

With love from Co-Pastor Lauretta McCoy Baldwin
and Contributing Authors

Lady Penny Hauser
Co-Pastor Lisa Hill
Pastor Sandra Samuels
Lady Mechelle Hayes
Lady Lauren Thomas
C.P.R.
Lady Michlin Bailey
Pastor Heatherly Price
Lady Annette Hairston
Lady Tujuana Bailey Barr
First Lady Demetraus Austin